TOUCHED BY GRACE

The Journey

To Giselle,
Abundant
graces to you!..
Amdguid

Anna Maria De Guid

ISBN 978-1-64349-677-1 (paperback)
ISBN 978-1-64458-729-4 (hardback)
ISBN 978-1-64349-678-8 (digital)

Cover and book design by Isabella Ramos
Editing by Josh B. Francia and Isabella Ramos

Christian Faith Publishing, Inc.
832 Park Avenue
Meadville, PA 16335
www.christianfaithpublishing.com

Names of characters and some situations in the stories have been changed. The substance and message of the stories remain intact.

Printed in the United States of America

ACKNOWLEDGMENTS

I wholeheartedly thank family and friends who have been a part of this compilation.

I offer warm and sincere appreciation to those who have given their precious time to read the drafts, who have provided much-needed advice, comments and suggestions, and who have proffered enthusiastic support. I am immensely indebted to those who have helped me comb through my edits.

Above all, I thank God for opening my heart to see his graces and for giving me the privilege to write and share these stories with you.

CONTENTS

INTRODUCTION

H as something ever happened to you that made you think, "What a coincidence!" How about incidents that have come up and made you say, "What a pleasant surprise!" Or maybe there had been something unexpected that touched your heart so much that it seemed to overflow with joy.

How about situations that made you feel as if there was no one listening to your prayers and pleas—when everything seemed to go wrong without any end in sight, and you just hung in there. Then after years of wanting and waiting, the pieces of the puzzle suddenly perfectly fit, and a whole new understanding dawns on you.

Most of us probably have had these experiences. Most likely, we have acknowledged the event and moved on with our busy daily lives.

I have had these occurrences on numerous occasions, so much more than the forty stories in this compilation, and I could not help but think that there must be more than just coincidence or luck. I would much rather think of these as an orchestration of events subtly guiding me, prodding me to see God's grace in my life.

The first two decades of my family life were spent sharing recipes and food with family and friends—food that nourished bodies, food that celebrated the holidays, food that tingled our taste buds and opened up new and exciting culinary worlds.

The early part of the third decade, however, directed me to share something that would nourish more than just the body. It was still a pleasure to prepare dishes, but with it came a desire to share things satisfying to more than just the palate and tummies.

This time, there was a wish to share something that would lighten the heart and nourish the soul.

THE JOURNEY TO WRITING

There are various ways God "talks" to us to let us know his plans for us. It could be through reading the Bible, through dreams, or maybe through whispering to the heart. God is all-knowing, and since he figured that I am a clueless person, he had to let me know in no uncertain terms.

1974.

"You will write."

The words were as clear as can be. The thing was, those words were spoken in my mind. Only I "heard" them. I was staring at the slowly burning candle adorning the tombstone of my paternal grandparents in my parents' hometown in the Philippines when those three words were spoken.

It is traditional Filipino custom to spend All Saints' Day November 1 in the cemetery praying for the souls of the dearly departed. It is also a chance to see relatives whom we had not seen in exactly a year, in the same place.

I felt, as a teenager, that this tradition was an exercise in patience. After all, families usually stayed at the cemetery for half to the whole day and often until sunset. It was the pre-smartphone, iPod, and iPad era, so you can imagine what handful of things one could do within the confines of about a ten-square feet area.

"Me, write?" I sort of answered the "voice." No response there.

I remembered we had a creative writing class the following Monday at school, so I told myself I was going to give it my best shot. I was just so inspired by that voice. Maybe this could be my path. Maybe I was meant to be a journalist, maybe a novelist. I was a sophomore in high school, and I only had a vague idea of what college was about. Other classmates already had a sense of what they wanted to be: an accountant, an actuary, an architect... And that's just the start of the alphabet! I can't imagine what other careers and professions others had in mind.

The following day Tuesday, our papers were returned. "Ugh!" I grimaced at my grade, "That's it!" I was so extremely disappointed with my grade that the thought of becoming a writer was immediately tossed out the window. I expected at least an A-.

Well, I also got the lowest spelling score in the class, so I thought it was best to stay away from writing. (Thank heavens for Spell Check feature of word processors these days!) That's one path I crossed out in my mind, among the vastness of choices open to me.

A couple of years later, an insanely embarrassing situation hammered the final nail into the writer's coffin. (I have kept this secret all these years. Not even my husband knows my mortifying story!)

And I did stay away from writing, except to keep in touch with family and friends and to write down recipes so I won't forget my culinary experiments.

1980s

I thoroughly enjoyed baking and wanted to enter culinary school, but never had the courage.

My dad had other plans for me. Don't get me wrong. I was thankful for his vision, as I had none. I wanted to pursue home economics, but Dad asked me to remove the "home" part and go for an economics degree. So I did.

During my single blessedness, I was arrogant and stubborn, thinking I knew everything. Those were the rainy and stormy days. Though I prayed about everything, I wanted to handle the wheel of the life I was living.

1990s

After I got married and had children, priorities changed drastically. I turned over the wheel to Jesus, although I did occasionally ask him to lend me the wheel.

That was when unusual events that I could not explain with logic started happening more frequently. Initially, I thought they were just coincidences, some wonderful, some painful but always ending with a deep sense of awe.

2014

I started scribbling notes to remember these events, and in early October of 2014, a relentless desire to share these stories overwhelmed me so much that I started to write about my experiences. It took me three weeks to finish thirty short stories with several still uncompleted ones.

At this time, I kept bumping into people whose careers were in publishing. I met a lady who edits articles for a Catholic publication. She offered to read my stories, and having read them, told me, "Prayerfully consider submitting your stories to a Catholic publication." She said my stories were very inspiring.

I was not familiar with any Catholic magazine that published short stories. Because I was an avid Guideposts reader, I submitted one of my stories to the magazine one fateful day in late October. Upon submission through the Internet, the magazine's general response was,

> *"Thank you. Your submission has been received. You will only be notified if your article has been accepted for publication either in the magazine or on the site. If you have not heard from us in two months, feel free to submit your story elsewhere."*

As the two months seemed to drag and passed, I prayed to Jesus, "You know I submitted my story because I truly believe the story was a grace from God. The only reason I wrote my stories was I felt God wanted me to share his message of love to everyone." There was no hint of disappointment that my story was not accepted.

On the afternoon of December 31, 2014, my son Chris came running to me, "Mom! I forgot to tell you that someone from New York called about your story!" At that precise moment, I thought that a fire could bring our house down, and I would still be smiling.

Thank God that did not happen.

2015

Guideposts published my story!

I profusely thanked God for allowing me to share my story with so many people. That was what I needed to start polishing my other stories.

Months passed, and procrastination got the better of me until a gentle nudge and an eye-opening push from above told me it was time to move forward.

I woke up around 4:00 a.m. on November 22, 2015. I pulled Mom's *Daily Bread* prayer book, and I flipped to the reading for that day. It was from Romans 12:6:

"Having then gifts differing according to the grace that is given to us, let us use them."

The narrative related to the reading discussed the life of C. S. Lewis, who converted to Christianity as an adult. He used his gift of writing to spread the gospel of Jesus.

Four days later, our family went to a Thanksgiving dinner upon an invitation of a family friend in Los Angeles. I had the for-tuity of sitting beside an out-of-town guest. She was relating the challenges she and her family faced as they moved to New Mexico to fill a special education teaching post. As she mentioned that it was through God's providence that they made it through tough times, I took a moment to share with her my story of grace.

I was beginning to tell her about my son who won the first-grade spelling bee when her eyes widened and she asked, "Are you the author of *that* story?"

"Oh, you read my story in Guideposts!" I was delighted that I now knew someone outside my circle of family and friends who read my story.

"No... I heard your story from a speaker at a special education convention in New Mexico!"

I could not believe what I was hearing. Neither did she.

Right there, I knew I had to share my stories. C. S. Lewis was the gentle nudge, and meeting this woman was God's eye-opening push.

2016

On New Year's Day, I firmly resolved to finish my compilation of short stories by mid-year. Slowly and with a lot of subconscious hesitation, I completed my draft. (Who was I to write these stories? I had to remind myself that these stories were not mine. They were handed down to me to share.)

I was so excited that I finally finished the compilation and was going to send a copy to an online publishing company when the thought hit me: *What's the title going to be?*

I spent the next couple of days brainstorming some possible titles: *A Journey of Grace, Grace Abounds, God's Everyday Grace, Our Daily Grace.* Nothing seemed right. On the second day, as I was thoughtlessly walking around the house, a picture of a book flashed in my mind: *Touched by Grace.* I saw the book in my head! Excitement and astonishment filled me, but only for a few days.

Weeks passed, and I put my plans of Do-It-Yourself online publishing on hold. Again.

In June 2016, I had the opportunity to visit the Philippines. My sister, who was also in Manila, submitted a manuscript to a publishing company there and was going to meet with the staff for the final editing of her book.

"If you have time, do join me." My sister's invitation was a wonderful occasion to catch up on each other's lives.

At the publishing house, while waiting for her meeting to finish, a family spiritual mentor asked me what I have been doing lately. I shared my stories of mysterious coincidences. The stories must have impressed him because, within a few minutes, he called a publishing house staff member to talk to me. Before I had an idea of what was even happening, she presented me with a copy of a contract!

Throughout this journey, there's been one grace after another, a grace within a grace, and just about a sprinkling of grace everywhere.

I once asked a friend, "How do you know what God's plan is for you?"

She replied, "Wherever the road opens, that is his plan for you."

There was a road that was beckoning.

It just needed some time to reach.

1974-2014.

Forty years.

In God's time.

"For I know well the plans I have in mind for you
-Oracle of the Lord- plans for your welfare and not for woe,
so as to give you a future of hope."
-Jeremiah 29:11

JOURNEY TO PUBLISHING

One of the many beautiful things with aging for me is the patience that has been nurtured through the years. I used to want things right away. Not anymore.

I had been presented a contract to publish my stories in the Philippines in 2016. I was ecstatic!

Then came the waiting part.

"So what's taking your book so long to publish?" my sister asked. "It's been almost a year."

"I have no idea," I replied. "In God's time."

I have to admit, though, I was asking myself why it was taking longer than I thought. But then I didn't know anything about publishing, so maybe that's how long it normally takes to publish a book.

One evening, I was surfing the Internet to learn more about the publishing process when something popped out—"Free Publication Kit." Being a freebie fanatic, I pressed the button.

A literary agent from Christian Faith Publishing called the following day. I told her I had a manuscript that was being reviewed by a Philippine publisher.

"Have you signed a contract with them? If you have, we cannot work with you." The agent wanted to clarify what was going on.

"Oh, no… I have not signed anything. They have accepted my manuscript for publishing, but they have not gotten in touch with me for months now even after I've called and emailed them."

The agent strongly suggested that I send them my draft, and a review board will go over my manuscript. She said that in five days they would let me know their decision.

After praying for guidance, I submitted my manuscript.

In five days, on the one-hundredth anniversary of the Feast of Our Lady of Fatima, I received their email accepting my stories!

Shortly after, I signed the contract.

A few weeks later, I received an email from the Philippine publisher telling me to resubmit my manuscript and that they were ready to work with me. They said that many projects had kept them away from my book.

Had the Philippine publisher communicated with me their situation earlier, I would not have searched the Internet. I would have waited.

It was God's plan for me to publish in the United States.

**"your kingdom come, your will be done,
on earth as it is in heaven."
-Matthew 6:10**

FLUVIAL PARADE

We rarely think that a person passed away at the right time, at the right age. We often say, "He or she is too young." That is because our lives are on God's time. Only He will know when it is our appointed time.

Every year on the first Sunday of July in the town of Bocaue, Bulacan in the Philippines, the townspeople celebrate the Feast of the Holy Cross of Wawa. This celebration is highlighted by a colorfully decorated float carrying a replica of the Holy Cross of Jesus parading slowly down the Bocaue River.

The legend says that centuries ago, a woman was saved miraculously from drowning by an image of the big wooden cross floating along the flooded river in barrio Wawa.

The woman, as the story goes, was about to sink when she caught a glimpse of the image of the cross. She tried to take hold of it, but it moved farther. The woman followed the image until she clung to it and then was able to reach the riverbank safely.[1]

So it was that every year my parents would bring our family of five down to an uncle's cozy cabin near the river for a hefty

---

[1] Provincial Government of Bulacan, Philippines, "Bulacan, Philippines: Bocaue, Bulacan: History," Bulacan, 2007, https://www.bulacan.gov.ph/bocaue/history.php.

potluck lunch. From the hut, we watched the flashy speedboats and the slow-moving, elaborately festooned *bancas* glide down the river, alongside the float of the Holy Cross.

One particularly adventurous and generous uncle had a speed boat that he shared with anyone who wanted a splashing of fun, excitement, and lots of water.

"Let the children go in the boat!" I heard people looking for my sister and me. My brother was too little to join the fun. For some reason, my sister decided she did not want to go. It was my opportunity to be able to experience my first-speed boat ride! I recall being put on the boat, but for some reason, they decided to pull me out at the last minute.

While waiting for my turn to ride the boat, I played around the area, and then I heard a growing commotion.

"Salamat sa gracia ng Diyos! Salamat sa Mahal na Birhen!" ("Thanks to God's grace! Thanks to the Blessed Virgin!")

My parents came looking for me and hugged me tightly. "We're so glad we got you out! The boat capsized!"

Looking back, that was my first encounter with the word "grace."

**"My soul rests in God alone, from whom
comes my salvation. God alone is my rock and
salvation, my fortress; I shall never fall."
-Psalm 62:2-3**

IN GOD'S EYES

"The grass is greener on the other side."
Sometimes it takes something astonishing to
realize the beauty of what we already have.

I learned early in life that Filipinos regard Western culture as superior. They liked the American way of doing things, their independence, their assertiveness, and a lot of other Western things. Filipinos also liked Caucasian physical characteristics—height, high nose bridge, blond hair, and their natural green and blue eyes. (This was years before colored contact lenses were even a concept!) At least I knew I did. Especially the eyes. I liked the way their eyes are set deep on their lovely facial contours.

For years I yearned to have eyes as they did. People would often comment on how my eyes would be lost in laughter and, likewise, in big smiles. In pictures, my eyes would always end up being lines, like two dashes as in the arms of the letter T.

It seemed every God-given day was another chance for me to wish I had better-looking eyes. I could not accept how the principle of dominant traits in genetics should have to work in my case. (Both my parents had almond eyes. How's that for being Queen of Denial!)

In college, I was looking to open an account at one of the banks on campus. As I was waiting in line, I glimpsed a well-dressed man seated behind one of the huge desks beyond the transactions counters who started looking in my direction. He walked towards my line. My turn was up, and I was completing a deposit slip at the counter when the man came up beside the teller, behind my counter and blurted out,

"Your eyes are the most beautiful eyes I have ever seen." For what seemed like a really long time, he peered into my eyes like he was looking at Queen Nefertiti's eyes.

The teller working on my deposit gave the man an incredulous look and then turned his stare at me with a face that shouted, "What is this guy saying?" After all, there was nothing really special about my eyes.

Not to him, not to anyone around there.

But to God, it was as special, unique, and beautiful as every other person's eye in this whole wide world. And he wanted to make sure I knew that.

"Thanks be to God for his indescribable gift!"
-2 Corinthians 9:15

MY PRAYER OF RELINQUISHMENT

*It's good to know what one wants, to have goals,
to work hard, and to persevere in prayers to get
what one desires. Sometimes though, what we
want may not be what is best for us. We have to
trust in God enough to let go of our plans.*

"Time to get up!"

During our childhood, Dad would come up to our rooms to pull our blankets and pillows to wake us up before 6:00 a.m. daily.

"The early bird gets the worm" and "Early to bed (not usually followed) and early to rise makes a man healthy, wealthy and wise" were household slogans. It did not matter to Dad what time we went to bed the night before; he instilled in our young minds the importance of starting the day early.

My older sister, younger brother, and I woke up before sunrise for early breakfast and were sent to school soon after because everyone in the family had a morning carpool schedule. I was the first to be dropped off during high school because my school was closest to home. Always one of the first to arrive in school, I was able to explore its expanse without being distracted by early morning chaos.

One morning as I was roaming around the buildings, I heard faint, melodious singing wafting through the air. I followed the music, which led me to the reception area of the main building, and realized that the sound was coming from the second floor. I slowly climbed the wide stairways, which landed in front of a small chapel. It was filled with nuns celebrating the 6:30 a.m. mass with a few young students in attendance.

That first time, I stayed for only a few minutes. As days and weeks passed, my few minutes later progressed to staying the entire mass.

After mass, I stayed behind and prayed for my only dream: for a good marriage and happy family life. I asked Jesus and the Blessed Virgin Mary for this one wish in my young life. I did not remember having asked for a successful career, for fame, for winning the lottery, or for some other wish…only that my knight would sweep me off my feet, and we would have a family and live happily ever after. (I think I read and watched too many fairy tales as a child.)

Months turned to years, which turned into decades with nothing to show for it. My dream of marriage and family was slowly fading away. Things had not turned out the way I wanted, though I truly believe I tried.

I was turning thirty-one when I dropped by St. Basil's Catholic Church in Los Angeles one August afternoon. I dropped down on my knees and opened my heart and mind to Jesus, though I was sure he already knew what was coming…

"You know all these years I have always prayed for a good marriage and happy family life, but it doesn't seem that this is what you have intended for me." With utmost humility and sincerity, I prayed, "If you have other plans for me, thy will be done."

When God closes a door, he opens a window.

I was astonished at these words that were distinctly spoken in my mind, something like telepathy. The words were spoken very clearly, not in the least vague or ambiguous. The words slowly settled peacefully in my mind, even if I did not quite understand then what they meant.

I left the church and continued with my life. October came, and the week before Thanksgiving, I was introduced to Paul. I don't remember having been swept off my feet, but the wondrous days of Christmas seemed to become more colorful that year, and by December 31, I felt that maybe, just maybe, God's knight had finally arrived.

Postscript: Fast-forward two decades later, I have Paul and three more charming knights: Andrew, Chris, Alex. And a happy family for which I am deeply and daily thankful.

"Rejoice always. Pray without ceasing.
In all circumstances give thanks,
for this is the will of God for you in Christ Jesus."
-1 Thessalonians 5:16-18

A SPELLING BEE M-I-R-A-C-L-E

"**M**om, can I bring *two* chicken legs for lunch?" my 6-year-old son AJ asked, smiling sweetly at me. I sighed. My son always made me proud—he'd recently been selected as one of two first graders to compete against two second grade students in the school's spelling bee—but I wished he wasn't such a picky eater. After all the delicious, healthy lunches I made for him came back to me uneaten, I'd finally given in and packed one of his favorite foods—a fried chicken leg. I was hoping he'd tire of it quickly—now he wanted two?

"Are you really going to eat two chicken legs?" I asked.

"One's for Kyle," he explained. His lunch buddy. Kyle usually bought lunch from the school cafeteria. How nice of my son to think of someone else! For the rest of the week, I packed him two chicken legs, impressed by his generosity.

Kyle's mom called that weekend to thank me for AJ's kind gesture. We got to talking about the spelling bee. "Does AJ know how to spell 'beautiful'?" Kyle's mom asked.

Beautiful? I had no idea. Why that word? Did she have some inside information? "No, nothing like that," Kyle's mom said. "It just popped in my head." Amused, I called AJ over and asked him to spell it. B-E-U-T-I-F-U-L… he missed the silent "a."

In the days leading up to the spelling bee, I drilled AJ on his words. I made a point to throw "beautiful" into the rotation. He kept getting it wrong. If AJ couldn't spell that word, did he have much of a shot at winning the bee?

The big day arrived. My husband and I took our seats in the school auditorium. I felt as nervous as AJ looked up on the stage. He spelled his first word correctly, then his second and third. His opponent had one word left to spell.

"The word is… 'beautiful,'" the announcer said.

I held my breath. AJ's eyes grew wide. Even wider when his opponent fumbled over the word and misspelled it. My son couldn't stop smiling as he finally nailed the word he'd been practicing all week.

All thanks to a chicken leg. One B-E-A-U-T-I-F-U-L act of kindness.

"Gifts clear the way for people,
winning access to the great.
-Proverbs 18:16

FROM CONDO TO FIRST HOUSE

This is a story on persevering in prayer. We cannot always have what we want. And if God is to give us what we desire, it takes a lot of coordinating people and events, which takes time, patience, and coincidences.

Paul and I moved into our first home in the early nineties. It was a one bedroom condominium unit in the outskirts of Los Angeles, California.

I loved our home and its location—it was close to almost everything, and the unit was perfect for a new couple.

I was able to walk along major commercial streets where banks and businesses offices were located. It had coffee shops, bakeries, and mom-and-pop stores interspersed between large business offices. There was a department store that had all the things I needed for special occasions. Then for food staples and other pantry supplies, there was a grocery close by. When we had our first child, I walked him to these places and had no need for another car. We lived simply and were content until …

Our living room started filling up with storage boxes. I covered the boxes with tablecloths or sheets so as not to direct attention to them when visitors came. I moved the few pieces of furniture we had to make the interior a little more appealing to the senses. I even took an interior design course to learn about scaling, color, harmony, and other design concepts.

But there's a limit to what creativity can do, especially if you have a little one with an expanding wardrobe and toy collection that grew with each birthday and holiday. When the piled boxes became taller than Paul, I knew we had to move.

Paul wanted to sell the condo before buying our home. Now, that was a little challenging because condominiums for sale were a hundred a block. Banks were also very strict about mortgages and were giving home buyers a hard time with loan applications. Nevertheless, we priced the condo so well that in less than a week, a buyer came forward to buy our property. Since we were selling on our own, we worked with the buyer and received regular updates on his loan application. After a few months of going back and forth with the bank, the buyer came to the house.

"I am sorry we decided not to proceed with the purchase. The bank that owns your mortgage is giving us a very difficult time. We completed all the paperwork and submitted all their requirements three times, and the bank lost our papers each time. You are very good people, but I am sorry to say that you will not be able to sell your condo. Your bank does not want to cooperate."

My heart sank. Paul did not want to pay two mortgages. The timing had to be exact. We needed to sell our unit, find a home, and close escrow on both transactions at the same time.

We resorted to the only thing we had left: *we prayed hard.* I remembered someone said that if we needed help with big things, then we needed to say big prayers.

The real estate market was at a junction where the overall market had started to recover from a recession but had not picked up speed yet. Some areas had started their upward momentum, and multiple offers on homes were beginning to show up.

That year, we made written offers on six homes, but none had been accepted because someone always beat us with a better offer. I was getting desperate and scared that the market might move up so fast that it would leave us unable to afford something we liked.

One Sunday evening, I was reading the *Los Angeles Times* and saw an advertisement by Downey Savings for mortgage loans. The following day, I called the bank for loan prequalification and was referred to loan officer Jesse M., who was kind enough to listen to our situation.

"What's your condo's bank and loan number?" Jesse asked. "Let's see what I can do about this." After I gave him the information, he said he would call as soon as he figured out something.

The following day, I received a call. "You won't believe this." Jesse was undoubtedly very excited about his news. "The loan officer handling your account was the best man at my wedding! He said he would do what needs to be done."

A few days after, another buyer Jesse C. made an offer on our condo and started the loan process with our loan officer's best man.

That same week, I saw an ad in the papers for a traditional ranch in the Royal Woods area. The home's price had once again dropped significantly. "Paul, I think we should look at this one." I called the agent and scheduled to view the house first thing in the morning.

Ecstatic to say that we sold our condo, bought our first home, and closed both escrows in the same month. The timing could not have been any better.

As we were signing final papers, Paul stared at me and said, "Do you find anything unusual in our transactions?"

Before I even had a chance to think, he answered, "The loan officer and our buyer's names are the same—Jesse."

I have no doubt someone up there was behind all the orchestration necessary for us to get exactly what we wanted.

"Blessed are those who trust in the LORD;
the LORD will be their trust."
-Jeremiah 17:7

ONLY THROUGH GOD'S GRACE

*To get angry, to want to get even after some-
one hurt us is normal human emotion. Maybe
instead, we should strive for something better
since we were created in the image of God.
Maybe we should pray for ourselves to be
granted the grace to forgive. That was exactly
what I did. And did it set me free!*

"**P**arents of Slain Child Forgive Murderer"

The headline popped out of the day's paper that I was reading.

I could never do that! I could never forgive the murderer!
My thoughts were filled with the details of the gruesome mur-
der. I couldn't even imagine forgiving a high school classmate
and college associate who had put me through years of subtle, but
effective verbal put-down. As the years progressed, my relationship with her continued to deteriorate.

I finally stopped communicating with her soon after college
graduation. Though she would get in touch occasionally, I would
be amicable, but cold. My deep-rooted resentment, the feeling of
wanting to get even in some way, and the heaviness in my heart
were alive, well, and kicking.

The classmate whom I will call Desiree grew up spoiled by
her admission. As such, she usually got whatever she wanted.
Everyone who knew her tolerated her behavior. Her friends knew
that her complaining and mean demeanor were a result of unre-
solved unhappiness in her life.

It was only through prayers that I was able to get through the
most challenging situations. Whenever they arose, I prayed with

almost every breathing moment. *Lord, please help me find peace with Desiree.* It seemed my life was consumed with the negativity that she brought into my life. Why did I allow this to happen? I don't know.

One Friday morning, as I was getting out of bed to start my work routine, I could not move. My entire body felt so heavy it seemed like an anchor was pinning my body down, and at the same time, my muscles felt too weak to be able to counter the massive weight. My body temperature was normal, and I had neither aches, nausea, or vomiting. I just felt immobile.

"I never thought that the physical manifestations of depression could be this bad." I agonized at the thought. I called in sick.

Saturday came, and there was no improvement. I stayed in bed the whole day, not knowing exactly what was going on. I decided to go to the clinic for a checkup the following Monday.

Early Sunday morning, I dragged my body to get a glass of water. As I turned and faced the kitchen window, the morning sun hit my face, and at that precise moment, I felt a miraculous release of all my resentment and bitterness towards Desiree. Every ill feeling faded into nothingness. A feeling of lightness in my heart, mind, and body ensued.

Desiree remained the same. Now it just became transparent how sad she must feel inside, and what was once resentment was now deep compassion and understanding for her.

Thank God, forgiveness has finally come to me. Now it's time to pray for God's grace to bless Desiree.

> **"For by grace you have been saved through faith,**
> **and this is not from you; it is the gift of God;**
> **it is not from works, so no one may boast."**
> **-Ephesians 2:8-9**

SPECIAL DELIVERY

Have you thought about how amazingly fast things are being delivered these days? I remember the days when domestic mail took a week, and international mail took two to three weeks. These days are the age of two-day, next day, and overnight deliveries. Can anyone beat that?

"**I**'m in a bind," Lita began her call, "Money I've been expecting has not arrived, and I have a check that's coming in on Friday that I have to cover. Do you think you can lend me some money that I'll pay off the next few weeks?" Though I could sense the desperation in her voice, I did not think Lita was in any huge dilemma. Her faith was so solid and strong that whatever challenging circumstances she had, she was going to meet them head-on.

Lita was a good and dear friend. Though she lived quite a distance from us in Florida, we kept in constant touch through the ups and downs of life. I could not let her down. It was summer, so our tuition woes had not yet kicked in.

"When do you need it?" I knew my husband wouldn't mind.

"If you mail the check tomorrow Monday morning, then I should get it by Friday. That should cover the incoming check," she replied.

That evening, I wrote Lita a card, and Paul inserted the check inside. I made sure Paul mailed the check early the next day before going to work. "She said she needed it," I hollered to Paul as he left for work Monday morning.

As always, time took flight, and on Wednesday evening, Lita called, "I received your card, but it had no check."

"That can't be. I saw Paul put in the check. Are you sure?"

Lita was getting a little agitated. "It's not here, not inside the card. I've been working extra hours, and the house is a mess. I might have put the check somewhere. Would you please, please send me another check? I'll cancel the first one if ever I see it." There were only a few times I've heard Lita sound as distraught.

The following day Thursday morning, Paul dropped off the second check at the post office via priority mail during his 10:00 a.m. break time. I even called him to make sure that he didn't forget to mail the check.

Around 3:00 p.m. the same day, Lita called with a jovial voice that was a world apart from this morning. "That was sure fast! I just came from the post office and got your check!"

"What you probably have is the first check because Paul just mailed the second check this morning."

"No," Lita said, "I just came from the post office and was opening your envelope when I called. What's the check number Paul issued this morning?"

"Oh, my goodness!" I was astounded. "It's the same check that Paul mailed earlier today!" The same check mailed from California at 10:00 a.m. arrived in Florida before 3:00 p.m.!

I heard a soft sobbing at the other end of the line. We both knew the USPS did not deliver this time.

Postscript: After three months, Lita called, "I found the first check."

"Rejoice, you righteous, in the Lord;
praise from the upright is fitting.
Give thanks to the Lord on the harp;
on the ten-stringed lyre offer praise."
-Psalm 33:1-2

CORRIE AND HER PENTHOUSE

Has anyone told you how marvelous heaven is?
According to family and friends who have passed
and have come back to life, it is just incredibly
beautiful. I have read identical descriptions from
people who have written about their near-death
experiences.[2] If people from everywhere around
the world have described the same experience
with similar words, it's hard not to believe.

My sister Rosie often had dreams of Dad, Mom, and other departed family members. I don't mind not having those dreams because I easily get scared, and when I dream, the images stay with me for a very long time.

Corrie was a first cousin on my father's side. She came to Los Angeles with her sister Ces in the seventies to try their luck. Both sisters were very entrepreneurial. Over their first decade in California, they started successful produce markets and fast-food health bars in Santa Monica, Venice, and Marina del Rey. In achieving this, they were able to help their family in this country of unlimited opportunities.

When I first came to Los Angeles, Corrie and Ces opened their hearts and home to me. Well, they opened their hearts and home to anyone who was visiting. It was part of their family values to extend help whenever they can.

---

[2] Eben Alexander, *Proof of Heaven: A Neurosurgeon's Journey into the Afterlife*, First Edition (New York: Simon & Schuster, 2012); Mary C. Neal, *To Heaven and Back: A Doctor's Extraordinary Account of Her Death, Heaven, Angels, and Life Again: A True Story*, First Edition (Colorado Springs: WaterBrook, 2012).

In the eighties, I decided to migrate here to the U.S. I stayed with Corrie for a few months before I ventured out on my own. During the time I lived with her, I discovered how incredibly wonderful a person she was. Her every fiber was made of generosity, honesty, empathy, and more generosity.

As I moved on with my life, she regularly called to update me on her family and also to ask how I was doing.

So it was very devastating when I learned that she was diagnosed with pancreatic cancer at the young age of fifty-five. I recalled it was sometime October when she came to visit me.

"You know I lost ten pounds last month. I think I am still losing weight rapidly."

"How?" I asked.

"I don't know. I don't have the appetite."

Not having an appetite was an experience unknown to me, so I pressed, "How's that?"

"Food just tastes like rust." Now that answer was unforgettable. I called my sister, who is a physician and told her about Corrie's condition. With a grave and sinister voice, she said, "Tell her to get a checkup as soon as possible. I think it's cancer."

Corrie was soon diagnosed with an aggressive pancreatic cancer after her doctor's visit, and in seven months, she was gone. Days after she passed, in my daily thoughts, I wondered how she was doing. I had no question where she was. I was missing her.

One night I had one of the most vivid dreams I ever had.

It was evening, and only the stars brightened the night sky. I was on the rooftop of an amazing penthouse adorned with the most beautiful orchids you can imagine. Around the entire perimeter and scattered all over the penthouse were these exotic flowers of every vibrant color. Having been an orchid enthusiast for years, I was amazed at her collection.

"I need to take pictures of you and your place to show back home." I did not know that she had passed away in that dream. It was as if she were still alive and just showing me her new house.

She answered, "Come join us, and let someone else take the picture."

"No, I'll take it. Okay now… 1…2…3." And with that camera click, I woke up.

I have no doubt that Corrie is in heaven, somewhere where everything, especially flowers, was in their most brilliant colors.

This was one dream I do not mind keeping for a very long time.

"Blessed are those who dwell in your house!
They never cease to praise you."
-Psalm 84:5

PAUL AND THE SDB

I believe that our dearly departed, who have accepted Jesus as their Savior, will spend eternity in heaven, just like the man on the cross who died beside Jesus. And I think that those who have lived their lives according to God's will shall be given special graces in heaven. Maybe they will be given the opportunity to help people on earth with their needs, much like angels do.

"**I** wonder what happened to the safety deposit box (SDB) that *Lola* and I opened in Santa Rosa," Paul was thinking aloud. He was toying with a key that reminded him of the bank's safety deposit box.

"I remember leaving some things in that box, and I think this might be the key. I don't quite remember the number of the box. Just that it was with one of the commercial banks in the town."

"This is going to be like looking for a needle in the haystack." He sighed. "Maybe I can get information from *Ninang* on our next visit to Manila."

Lord, this is not going to be easy, I whispered to myself.

In the eighties, Paul opened a safety deposit box in Santa Rosa, a town in the province of Laguna in the Philippines. *Lola,* his maternal grandmother, was the co-signer of the box. After she passed in 1980, he soon left for Los Angeles. He was nineteen, and the box had not been opened since.

Paul and I met during the 1990 Thanksgiving season and married in 1992. He had not mentioned anything about the safety deposit box until that day.

"So what's the plan?" I asked Paul.

"Well, it's not much of a plan. I want to drop by *Ninang* to ask her about the box. I'll borrow the keys to *Lola's* room in the ancestral home. I might find something in her room that would give me the information I need."

"But it's been a decade… How sure are you that your box is still in the bank?" I inquired.

"I'll ask *Ninang* next time we visit the Philippines."

That summer, we visited my parents in Manila and scheduled a trip to Santa Rosa. We met Paul's godmother *Ninang,* who had been keeping the rental payments to a box that she had never looked into. Paul borrowed the key to *Lola*'s room and left for the ancestral home.

It wasn't long before he returned with such bewilderment on his face.

"You will not believe this…" Paul announced with eyes as baffled as his voice. "As I opened *Lola's* room, the first thing I saw was a paper lying on the middle of Grandma's untouched bed. It was the safety deposit box receipt! There were no other papers anywhere around. The entire room looked frozen in time!" The paper was flat, tainted brown from age, but all the information was very clear.

It was dated March 26, 1980.

**"And he said, 'What is impossible for
human beings is possible for God.'"
-Luke 18:27**

LAST MINUTE CHANGE

*There may be several things we can control, but
many more variables we cannot. Like our innate
personality. And the world around us. Thank God
that he knows us and knows what is best for us.*

I believe I was born with an out-of-this-world imagination and an
easily agitated, excitable personality. And grew up with an endless
string of worries alongside a ton of anxieties. There's not much to
add to that to create a panic-stricken persona. The only way I was
able to cope with all these was through unceasing prayers. *Lord,
please protect our family, keep us safe, and guide us always.*

Such was my state-of-being when I got married. I had
thoughts of someone breaking into our home while my husband
was working the night shift. That was why my aunt stayed with me
whenever Paul worked late hours.

I was five months pregnant with my first child, and Auntie was
supposed to stay with me the evening of January 16. She called me
in the afternoon to ask if I felt secure being by myself because she
was staying that evening with a friend who was visiting Los Angeles.

"That's fine, Auntie," I replied, positive that I could handle
all those creepy little thoughts.

It was almost 10:00 p.m. when the phone rang. It was Auntie
calling.

"Is it okay for me to stay with you tonight? My friend had
made other plans and forgot about the sleepover."

It was late at night when she came, and I went back to sleep.

It was still dark when Auntie and I were awakened by the
sudden jolt brought about by an earthquake that seemed to go on

forever. The lamps shook, the dry goods fell off the pantry, and our third-floor unit just seemed to sway indefinitely. The TV fell from its stand while the glass sliding doors and mirrors seemed like they were about to be dislodged.

We were making our way toward the elevator when one of the residents came out and told us that the building was strong enough to withstand those jolts as it has survived worse earthquakes. He suggested we stay inside.

As Auntie and I went back to the unit, I couldn't imagine what a wreck I would have been if I were alone that evening.

Twenty-two years later, this is what is known of the earthquake:

> *The Northridge earthquake that struck at 4:31 a.m. on Monday, January 17, 1994, affected an area of 2,192 square miles in the San Fernando Valley, a densely populated residential area of northern Los Angeles, California. In terms of financial losses, Northridge is one of the worst disasters in US history.*[3]

"Be strong and steadfast; have no fear or dread of them, for it is the LORD, your God, who marches with you; he will never fail you or forsake you."
-Deuteronomy 31:6

---

[3] William J Petak and Shirin Elahi, "The Northridge Earthquake, USA and Its Economic and Social Impacts," *EuroConference on Global Change and Catastrophe Risk Management Earthquake Risks in Europe, IIASA, Laxenburg Austria, July 6-9, 2000*, 2001, 28.

ANDREW FALLS OFF HIS CRIB

One very early morning, our second floor neighbor called, asking if I heard a blood-curdling scream past midnight. I said I didn't hear anything. She was wondering what could have caused the nightmarish scream. Our neighbor passed years later. From heaven, she now knows who did it.

I believe in angels, but have I ever seen one?

When I gave birth to my first child, I decided to breastfeed him. One of the challenging things for me about breastfeeding came from sleep deprivation. The milk got digested faster and made the baby hungry after just a couple of hours. I would breastfeed Andrew at 7:00 p.m., and soon after, he would wake up craving for his next feeding.

One morning shortly after midnight around 2:00 a.m., I was awakened by crib, sheet, and toy sounds all symphonizing together to what we call noise. Andrew was holding on to the crib rails, trying to stand up.

Upon standing, he tried to reach out for a toy that fell on the floor. My eyes were half open, and I was trying to keep my eyelids up. My mind told me, "You need to get Andrew... You need to get Andrew"... but my body was just following the principle of inertia: a body at rest tends to stay at rest. Our bed was parallel and about three feet away from the crib. I was looking directly at Andrew from our bed and thinking that he would probably give up trying at some point.

A split second later, I saw Andrew's body somersault over the crib with his head on the crib handle, and his entire body turned upside down in midair!

I heard a blood-curdling shrill come out of me! Instantaneously, I saw what seemed to be a blurry white sheet, like a wispy thin cloud, cover my view of Andrew.

The next thing I saw was that Andrew was on the floor, crying.

"Let's take him to the hospital!" I was so scared of the injuries Andrew might have sustained from the fall. Paul suggested we observe him for a few hours as he felt that Andrew was crying out of shock more than from pain.

Andrew soon quieted down after he was cuddled. I *prayed unceasingly* for normalcy for my son. I read somewhere that prayers of mothers for her children are those heard most in heaven. I made sure he did not sleep right away so that we could observe if there was any unusual behavior after the fall.

Everything seemed fine the days following the fall.

To this day, I still wonder what that white blur that covered my view of Andrew was. I want to think that it was his guardian angel, making sure that his fall will have a soft landing.

**"I looked again and heard the voices of many angels
who surrounded the throne and the
living creatures and the elders.
They were countless in numbers..."
-Revelation 5:11**

CHRIS'S BIRTH

A baby's birth is a highly awaited and celebrated event. For Caesarian delivery, the parents can choose their baby's special day. For natural born babies, birthdates are a guessing game. In some baby showers, the person who guesses the right delivery date will be given a prize. In some cases, the delivery date itself is the prize.

I had a very close and special relationship with Mom. When I migrated to the US, it was a very difficult time for me. In the eighties when mail was still the primary mode of written communication, I would write to her almost daily and call her as often as I could. Whenever I had great news, I would call her first: during my engagement, wedding, first home, first house, and my first pregnancy.

Then when I was thirty-eight, I became pregnant with my second child. I was scared, as any mother would be, since I was past the safe pregnancy years of the early and mid-twenties.

"Dear God, please grant us a healthy baby," was my daily prayer.

When my mother learned of my pregnancy, her wish was for me to have a girl since my firstborn was a boy.

"My child, pray for a girl. God will grant you a girl if you ask for one." During phone calls, she would say things like, "It's nice to have a girl. They usually stay with you and keep in touch more." I felt she wanted me to have a daughter with whom I could build a strong bond as I had with her.

After a few months when the amniocentesis results came out, Paul and I learned that we were going to have another boy. I don't remember having been let down in any way.

Mom was pretty disappointed with me. "That's because you did not pray for a girl." She was a prayerful woman of few words, and I knew how much she wanted me to have a girl.

One evening around my fourth month, Mom told me that she had a very lifelike dream. She dreamed she saw my baby with facial features that were unmistakably from the maternal side of the family: round facial contour, almond eyes, and a nose that was unmistakably ours. Our first born took after Paul's side of the family. She knew in her heart right then that it was God's plan for me to have a boy. I explained, "Mom, God's telling you that this baby is going to be special to you."

The second trimester turned to third, and on my ninth month, I was getting more anxious by the day. I had a very difficult twenty-two-hour labor with my first pregnancy and prayed that this would be different.

My due date, September 26 passed with a few false contractions. My parents and brother all flew from the Philippines to Los Angeles to surprise me, only to be surprised themselves that I had not yet given birth.

"Anna, cook this recipe and eat the whole thing in one sitting. I guarantee you will give birth the following day," advised a good friend. So I gave her recipe a try. I cooked her dish, which tasted very much like fruit cake cooked on a stove, and downed the whole pot of mushy fruit cake batter with what felt like a gallon of water.

I suppose that was the first time that her recipe did not deliver.

Every day I would walk the stairs, mop the floors, clean the house, and do just about anything that needed a lot of exertion.

Finally, October 8 came, and my water broke during the early morning hours. Paul brought me to the hospital, and that afternoon, I gave birth to a healthy, chunky, and almost eight-pound baby boy with features just like Mom saw in her dream.

And to top that, Chris was born on Mom's birthday too.

**"For everything created by God is good,
and nothing is to be rejected when received
with thanksgiving, for it is made holy by
the invocation of God in prayer."
-1 Timothy 4:4-5**

GRACES FROM THE ROSARY

I have petitioned so many favors from our Lord Jesus with the intercession of the Blessed Mother Mary. Blessings of safety, good health, protection, guidance, and so much more have been showered on my family and me.

And there were blessings that were not even asked for.

Pets all over the world hold a special place in the hearts of those who care for them and more especially so in the United States.

That's why I was horrified with every bit of my being and instinctively closed my eyes when Paul and I both felt the not-so-gentle hump as we drove over a Shih Tzu that suddenly crossed the bustling intersection of Seventh Street and Alvarado Boulevard in Los Angeles. The light turned green, and Paul stepped on the gas when the dog suddenly ran in front of us.

When I opened my eyes, I saw spectators' bewildered, shocked faces, some with hands on their mouths, as we feared the worst—to see the mangled body of the dog lying under the car.

"No!" I gave a muffled shout that only my heart could hear.

Then a couple of short seconds passed.

"Wait... I just saw the dog sprint from under our car and cross Alvarado!" Paul was just mystified by what he saw.

My heart leaped as I recalled the story of a couple who hit and ran over a young child who suddenly ran across their path.

"Paul, I can't believe this is happening to us. You see, there's a story about a couple who ran over a child, and the child had no injuries whatsoever! They were praying the rosary when the accident happened."

We were finishing our rosary when we hit the dog.

How I wish I could remember where I read that story.

Two months later, just before leaving for a trip, I grabbed a book that I had not finished reading. As I opened the book at the airport and started reading, I could not believe my "luck"! It was the very story I was looking for!

> *He stepped on the accelerator to assume normal speed. Suddenly, a little girl, maybe less than five years old, darted across our path. She was hit and caught under our vehicle.... To our great amazement, however, the child rolled out from under our vehicle to the other side of the street, alive and seemingly unharmed... I realized that my rosary was dangling from my hand. Tita Babe and I had been praying the Rosary during the trip.*[4]

**"With all prayer and supplication,
pray at every opportunity in the Spirit.
To that end, be watchful with all perseverance
and supplication for all the holy ones."
-Ephesians 6:18**

---

[4]   S. J. Fr James B. Reuter, *Mama Mary and Her Children (Book 3): True Stories of Real People*, Mama Mary and Her Children 3 (Mandaluyong City: Anvil Publishing, Inc., 2011).

ALEX AT KIDSPACE

I believe that bad things can happen to anyone, anytime. But I believe too that if we keep ourselves enveloped with God's sheath of protection and guidance, our innermost being will be able to discern things that cannot be revealed by our senses alone.

I was preparing my youngest son Alex's snacks for his kindergarten field trip that day *while praying for fun and his well-being.* I was not one of the chaperones and casually asked another mom Lisa where Kidspace Children's Museum was.

"Oh, it's very close to the Rose Bowl," Lisa answered. I thanked her and requested another mom to keep an eye on Alex.

"Does he eat anything?" Vicky asked. "I have cashews."

"He is very allergic to peanuts, so you can give him anything but those." And with those words, I hugged Alex and saw him get on the school bus. Shortly thereafter, the class left for Kidspace in Pasadena.

Paul and I were going to visit an aunt in the San Fernando Valley that morning. While preparing to go, nudging thoughts of checking on Alex came to me. "Alex was all set when I left him," I rationalized to those nagging thoughts. Still the idea of checking Alex one last time before we went to the Valley persisted.

And then a feeling of ambiguity, uncertainty, and urgency about Alex enveloped my entire being. I told Paul that I wanted to find Kidspace and check out Alex.

"I'm not sure he got his lunch bag," I explained, trying to find a reason to see Alex.

"He should be fine. Didn't you say that you saw Mrs. Fernandez put the students' lunch bags in a box?" Paul commented.

Nevertheless, I insisted that I had to see Alex, and after more convincing, Paul relented. We drove to the Rose Bowl in Pasadena, and as we looked for parking at the adjacent Kidspace Museum, we saw Alex with Vicky by his side. Alex was flustered, was coughing incessantly, and had difficulty breathing.

"The school has been trying to get hold of you but could not contact you," Vicky explained.

I just changed my phone and had not been able to update the school's emergency file. We thanked Vicky, excused Alex from the teacher, and drove home.

In the van, Alex was very restless and continued coughing until he started throwing up. In the house, he continued to expel everything he had eaten until he felt so tired that he just fell asleep.

Later that day, we brought him to the doctor's office, where the allergy specialists did some testing. When the results came out, it confirmed peanut allergy was his primary allergy, followed by cashews! My heart sank! If not for those nagging thoughts, things could have turned out bad.

That evening, while Alex fell asleep on my lap, I could not thank the heavens enough for the guidance that was given to me. Someone out there was watching out for our son.

"Do not let your hearts be troubled.
You have faith in God, have faith also in me."
-John 14:1

DÉJÀ VU

Parenting is probably the most difficult job. Parents give their unconditional love and best efforts, but the result of the child-rearing endeavor will not manifest itself until decades later.

My friend Sarah was driving and listening to a talk show host giving advice to callers. The topic was about parenting. One caller was a twenty-one-year-old young man who called to say that his parents were disciplinarians, but he saw, through his parents' conservative and regimented policies, their love for him. He said that he was so full of gratitude for all that his parents have done for him.

"It is rare for a man your age to appreciate his parents as much as you do," the host commented. "Often, parental appreciation never even comes."

Sarah was teary-eyed as she listened to the conversation.

"Wow," she thought, "The parents must have done really well to have brought up their child to see and appreciate what they have done." Her thoughts consequently flowed to her two sons, who were then in their pre-adolescent teenage years. She said it was a handful keeping her ground with them. She divulged that it was a real challenge, reasoning and answering all their "Whys?"

"Why can't we watch R-rated movies when all our friends have been watching them since grade five? Why can't we stay overnight at So-so's friend's house? Sarah disclosed that she let them win the battle often because she wanted to win the war. There were so many other issues with religion, culture, and even the importance of family and God. Sarah disclosed that she prayed every day that her sons would understand the reasons why she and her husband were being strict. She beseeched God to guide her sons.

Years passed, and her older son was a sophomore in college.

"One afternoon while I was driving home," Sarah continued, "Alan called me."

"Mom, I want you to know how much I appreciate the way you and Dad raised me. You had always supported me in what I chose to do in school, in my extracurricular activities, and even in my social life. I am so very blessed to have you and Dad as my parents."

"Anna," Sarah looked at me straight in the eye, "If a heart could burst with pure joy, mine would have at that moment."

Her son just turned twenty-one.

**"Enter his gates with thanksgiving, his courts with praise.
Give thanks to him, bless his name."
-Psalm 100:4**

TEACHER APPRECIATION

I believe people should be thankful for every-thing. Well, maybe, almost everything. Giving thanks makes me feel good. I know that thanks-giving releases the good hormones in our body that will help us lead better and longer lives. But this story is not about better and longer lives. It is simply letting people know that they are appreciated.

"How I wish the clouds and the smog would go away!" I was dismayed at the fuzziness of the day. The view from our backyard was great but not the way I wanted it to be for the day's celebration. I was longing for spectacular. The last few days, I was hoping and praying for windy weather to push the smog out and bring in the awesome beauty of a clear view.

God, if you will, please, please grant us a picture-perfect, clear day today, I prayed as I was putting the final touches to our outdoor gathering later that afternoon.

We were hosting our first and the last appreciation dinner for the school faculty in the backyard. The last of our three sons finally graduated from elementary school. All in all, our family has been with the school for fourteen years.

Throughout those years, I was in awe of the teachers who taught there, each having anywhere from twenty-five to thirty-five students per class. I could barely survive the hectic school day schedules of my three sons, and here they were all doing their best to teach our children academics and instill within them the values of Catholic education.

So when the time came to say our goodbye, Paul and I thought inviting our sons' teachers to our home as thanksgiving and appreciation for all their hard work would be a heartwarming gesture.

About an hour after the guests arrived, everyone was surprised when the clouds turned gray, and tiny droplets of an impending rain showered on the guests. Strong winds began blowing so hard that the tables and chairs had to be anchored. Guests squeezed to fit into the tents. This was the last thing I hoped would happen. We were all beginning to move the food trays inside the house when the guests said that the shower and winds suddenly stopped.

As I stepped out to return the food trays outdoors, my gaze was directed towards the horizon and what I saw was an incredibly clear, picture-perfect view of the Los Angeles city skyline and beyond!

Everyone marveled at the amazing views.

I was so filled with appreciation to God for giving us this unforgettable thanksgiving event, an affair that had an overwhelming sense of gratitude everywhere.

"The LORD has done great things for us;
Oh, how happy we were!"
-Psalm 126:3

PLANE ENCOUNTER

Auntie Lory gifted Paul and me a beautiful hand embroidered Our Lady of Lourdes picture encased in a frame, twenty-some years ago. I put it on my bedside night table, and it has stayed there ever since. We hadn't communicated with Auntie Lory in over a decade.

Two days before a flight to the Philippines, I finally got the push I needed to dust around the statuettes of my little bedside table. While I was wiping the Our Lady of Lourdes frame, I saw Auntie's handwritten card taped behind the frame, "Gift of Love, From Auntie Lory."

I wonder how she is doing. I thought. *I hope I remember to write her a card saying that her lovely gift is still with us. I will need to call people when I get back to Los Angeles to find her contact information.*

We had just settled in our plane seats en route to Manila when Paul tapped my shoulder and whispered, "The flight attendant beside you has Suarez on her nameplate."

I immediately called the attendant's attention.

"Are you related to the Suarezes of Bulacan?"

"My dad's Anthony," she responded.

"Any relation to Lory Suarez?" I excitedly blurted.

"She's my grandma!"

"I was just thinking about her!" I exclaimed.

I got a blank card from my bag, penned Auntie a note and asked the attendant to hand my card to her grandma.

As the plane took off, I muttered to Paul, "Couldn't believe how quick it was finding her!" Faster than any search engine and mail delivery anywhere.

"There is an appointed time for everything,
and a time for every affair under the heavens."
-Ecclesiastes 3:1

MOMENT OF TRUTH

There have been more than a handful of times when the day's gospel was exactly the theme that I had been pondering before attending mass. Jesus said, "I am the vine; you are the branches." It is during these times when I feel a powerful, heartfelt, and close connection to our Lord.

One of my favorite Bible passages was the part when Jesus went to the temple.

And the scroll of the prophet Isaiah was handed to him. Unrolling it, he found the place where it is written:

"The Spirit of the Lord is on me, because he has anointed me to proclaim good news to the poor. He has sent me to proclaim freedom for the prisoners and recovery of sight for the blind, to set the oppressed free, to proclaim the year of the Lord's favor."[5]

Then he rolled up the scroll, gave it back to the attendant, and sat down. The eyes of everyone in the synagogue were fastened on him. He began by saying to them, "Today this scripture is fulfilled in your hearing."

I could not get over this passage. Just how incredible could that scene at the temple be!

As I often try to do, I share bits and pieces of insightful talk with my youngest as I take him to school. (Nothing more than thirty seconds of these talks lest he falls into deep slumber never to wake up for school.)

---

[5] Lk 4:18-19

"Son, do you recall that passage where Jesus read from a scroll a prophecy about himself? That is one of my favorite passages. Can you imagine if you were there in the temple listening to the readings and in front of you stood this person who was a wonderment to everyone—as a teacher, a prophet, as the Messiah—and he read that passage?"

My son suddenly got sleepier. "Yes, Mom."

As I had the time to go to mass in the afternoon, I did, and to my total amazement, the gospel for that day was the scripture passage I shared with Alex that morning!

What a deeply powerful moment of truth.

"I am the vine, you are the branches.
Whoever remains in me and I in him, will bear much fruit,
because without me you can do nothing."
-John 15:5

A GENEROUS GIFT

*"Seek ye first the kingdom of God and his righ-
teousness. Then all these things shall be added
unto you. Alleluia!"[6] This story is a modern
take on the popular, well-loved church song.*

"**M**aybe you should get the flowers this weekend. It's
President's Day, and Home Depot or Lowe's might have some
good sales," my husband commented when I told him I was going
to get some plants for the church.

For weeks I had been asking myself if the church could use
more flowers. The church looked barren after the poinsettias were
removed after the Christmas season, and it did not feel right for
me. I am part of the group that cleans the church, and I thought the
church could use a little sprucing up, being God's house. I didn't
want to wait for the weekend sales to get the plants. *Never mind
the sale*, I thought. *A few dollars won't hurt.*

Using some spare time I had that Tuesday morning, I drove
to the nursery to see if I could find suitable potted plants for the
woven baskets that I purchased earlier.

I strolled around the aisles and aisles of potted foliage and
flowers; there were so many to choose from—beautiful variegated
foliage to blooming azaleas.

"I didn't expect choosing plants could be so time-consuming.
I need to hurry," I started talking to myself. I had an appointment
in about an hour and had to get going.

---

6   Karen Lafferty, *Seek Ye First* (Costa Mesa: Maranatha Music, 1974), https://
www.hymnal.net/en/hymn/ns/120

I finally decided on some purple campanulas and lavender chrysanthemums. I thought the colors were fitting as the Lenten season would begin in two weeks. I looked at my phone and saw that it was 10:00 a.m. I was running a tad late, so, hurriedly, I finished my purchase.

I drove straight to the church, arranged the plants in the baskets I previously bought, and placed them on the opposite walls. *There,* I mused. *Now that looks better.*

As I was leaving the church, my phone chimed. It was a text from our neighbor Marla. She said she just learned that a total of four people were not going to use their tickets to the corporate suite at Staples for that evening's Lakers game. She wanted to know if our family would like to join her.

I could not believe the invitation! Paul and our boys love watching the Lakers play. To watch a game at Staples Center. In a suite. As a family all together is a fabulous treat I could not have imagined! I called our neighbor as soon as I could, and not even thinking about my boys' schedules that evening, I accepted the invitation.

As I was going out the door for my appointment, my heart skipped a beat as a thought crossed my mind,

God is never outdone in his generosity.

Thank you, Lord, for this truly wonderful gift.

"Behold, I am coming soon.
I bring with me the recompense I will give to each
according to his deeds."
-Revelation 22:12

ASK AND YOU SHALL RECEIVE

I have petitioned our Lord for a lot of things.
Some of them took months, some a few years, and
a few of them even took decades to be realized.
So this petition was a pretty quick one for me.

"**A**lex, please choose between becoming a lector or an altar server," I asked my son which option he would prefer to volunteer at our church.

"Mom," he sheepishly answered, "may I clean the church instead?"

The elementary school children were required to do volunteer work as part of their school curriculum and being a shy one, Alex was not comfortable helping as an altar server or as a lector during Sunday masses.

Upon inquiring from the parish center, I learned that the chairperson of the church cleaning committee had relocated and had left the parish.

"Melinda, would you please have the new person in charge of the cleaning committee call me so Alex and I can start cleaning?" I asked the receptionist. A few days later, Melinda returned my call. "This may sound odd, but when I asked around for the person in charge, they gave me your name."

And that was how I offered to find parishioner-volunteers to work on a church that had not been cleaned for months.

The church doors were filled with grime and pitch black dirt. The holy water fonts had a discolored tint around the bowl, and the holy water seemed murky. The chandeliers looked like they had grayish cotton puffs sitting atop them.

Though the plants were fine and were probably being watered by caring parishioners, the counters had water and plant stains. The book, pamphlet, and brochure shelves had a powdery film of dust. The loft was so chalky that one could finger-write ones name on the rails, organ, pews, and chairs… and even on the memo boards!

I requested the parish office to run ads in the church's weekly bulletin, seeking for volunteers. After a few weeks, several parishioners called the parish office and left their contact information; however, no one ever responded to my telephone calls to schedule an orientation.

Weeks turned into months and though my son was fine, my back, shoulders, and arms were getting weary.

Once while dusting the shelves, I turned my eyes to Jesus at the altar and invoked, *Lord, if you would like me to continue in this ministry, I will stay and continue cleaning your house. But if you would like me to do other things for you, please send me some volunteers."*

The next two weeks that the church bulletin ran ads, six parishioners called to volunteer. And this time, they all showed up for the orientation.

To this day, the church has been blessed with this same group (and more) who cleans with all the enthusiasm, dedication, hard work, and love for our Lord.

**"Ask, and it will be given you;
seek and you shall find;
knock and the door shall be opened to you."
-Matthew 7:7**

INSTRUMENT OF GRACE

Maikki is a dear friend whom I see only once every couple of years, yet when we get together, it feels like we can just continue our stories from where we left off.

This time, did she have an unbelievably incredible new story to share!

Maikki is the third of five children. Her older siblings often stayed at her maternal grandmother's home while her younger siblings played with their cousins most of the time, so Maikki grew very close to her mom.

When her mother became very ill, she became her mom's go-to child. Maikki promised herself that she would hold her mom's hand if something serious happened to her. She thought that if her mom became incomprehensible, confused, or comatose, at least her mom might still feel her warm, comforting touch.

One afternoon, her mom had a heart attack while in the hospital for a follow-up visit. It was a blessing that all her siblings were there. The medical personnel rushed to her bed to start emergency procedures. Maikki stayed by her mom's side and steadily held her mom's arm. Out of the blue, her older brother brusquely pushed Maikki's arm away. She was shocked at his action, and her entire being instantly filled with rage at her brother's action. "If Mom dies now, I will never speak to him again," she told herself as she seethed in anger. As if her brother read her mind, he gently took her hand and put it back on their mother's arm.

Her mom survived the ordeal, but Maikki did not. She continued to be filled with anger and resentment towards her brother. For days, she did not talk to him. "It's a good thing Mom didn't die," she consoled herself. But still, she could not bring herself to speak with her brother again, even after all the praying she was doing to be able to forgive.

A couple of days later at her mom's house, she met the housekeeper, who asked, "Ma'am, how is your mother doing?"

"She's doing much better now. Thanks for asking." Maikki asked, "Do you still have your mom?"

The housekeeper related her story: "She died ten years ago. I grew up being closest to my mom. She was often sick, and I told myself that I would hold her hand if something really bad happened to her. I wanted her to feel that someone was comforting her."

She continued, "One day, Mom had a heart attack, and I held her hand in the hospital room while the doctors were trying to resuscitate her. All of a sudden, my brother brusquely pushed my hand away. Within a few minutes, my mom died. I was livid with anger at my brother. I felt that he was jealous of me because I was closest to my mother. Since then, I had not spoken to him. Even my children said that I have a hard heart and that I should already forgive. My brother has called me several times over the years to ask for forgiveness, but I would not take his calls."

Maikki was in shock at what she was hearing. She felt like the housekeeper was telling her, *her* story. All the feelings she had experiencd were being validated. It was justified and understandable how she felt. It took her more than a few minutes to gain composure.

"Ten years is a long time," she finally said. "Something could happen to your brother, and you might regret your actions. I think you should call him and reconcile. After all, he has been wanting to apologize."

The housekeeper was quiet for some time. "You are right," she finally replied.

That weekend, the housekeeper went to see her brother, and that was the first time their families got together after a decade of separation.

As for Maikki, she took her advice.

As for me, I am still wondering up to this time who the real instrument was.

> **"Come, let us sing joyfully to the Lord;**
> cry out to the rock of our salvation.
> **Let us come before him with a song of**
> **praise, joyfully sing out our psalms."**
> **-Psalm 95:1-2**

GERALDINE'S GIFT

This is such a heartwarming story that leaves one feeling joyful, awed, and inspired (to persevere in praying) all at the same time.

"**S**o, how's the family?" It was my usual opening question for Christine whenever I called her. Christine was a dear friend whom I treated like a sister.

"Oh, everyone's just the same. Well, everyone except Ben," she replied with a voice that had a hint of mystery. Ben was one of Christine's brothers.

"You know what he did? Out of the blue, he packed his bags, left his partner, and went back to the Philippines. Just like that. Did not tell anyone. In a week, he was gone."

"Why?"

"No one knew why."

A few years later, in Manila, I was attending a funeral when I bumped into Geraldine, Ben's wife. It was an opportunity to ask what happened to Ben. Here's Geraldine's story:

> "After Ben and I got married, we were struggling financially. I suggested that he relocate to the United States to find a job, get a permanent resident card, and petition me. With family in Los Angeles, we would have lots of support to help us get started. I thought the plan seemed easy enough. Ben didn't want to, but I was persistent, so with a heavy heart, Ben relented and left for California.

A few months later, I learned that a lady working with Ben fell in love with him, and the two started living together as husband and wife. I felt so much remorse as this plan was mine.

For ten years, I wrote to him regularly and sent him gifts on his birthdays, special occasions, and holidays. Ben never answered any of my letters, and all my gifts were returned. He just severed all forms of communication between us.

Since that happened, *I prayed unceasingly* every day to Jesus and the Blessed Virgin Mary for Ben. I attended weekly novenas at the Baclaran Church. Also, during that time, I continued to have difficulty making ends meet. I sold knick-knacks part-time for extra income.

Then one night, I had a dream that was so vivid I could still see, hear, and feel it in my mind. In that dream, Mother Mary appeared to me. She gently took my hand, lifted it closer to her, and asked me, 'My child, what do you want to ask of me?'

'Please bring me back Ben.' Despite my continued struggles with money, it did not even occur to me to ask for financial help. I did not think of anything else but Ben.

As soon as I had said those words, I suddenly woke up with my hands suspended in the air as if holding on to something. I burst into tears and cried until I could cry no more."

She paused and said, "The following week, Ben was beside me. Not only did Mother Mary grant me Ben. She also blessed us with Sofia the following year. You probably heard that I had problems conceiving when we got married."

I was speechless.

When I came back to my senses, I realized Ben did not have a child with the other lady despite having been with her for ten years.

"Rejoice in hope; endure in affliction, persevere in prayer."
-Romans 12:12

A FAVORITE HEALTHY SNACK

Have you ever felt a departed loved one make his or her presence known to you? That happened to me many times when my mother passed but rarely with my dad. This was one of his simple and subtle ways.

In the eighties, whenever I traveled, I would ask Dad what he wanted when I returned home to Manila. His answer would be Fig Newtons. *Hmmm, interesting,* I thought the first time he mentioned the Newtons. I haven't tried them, so I got a few packages—one for me to try and the rest for him.

After my first bite, I was hooked! It was a chewy and fruity snack that I thought had a perfect combination of sweetness and softness to it. It also sounded healthy.

Years passed, and Dad, a strong and fit man of seventy, was diagnosed with Alzheimer's. My sister, who was a medical doctor, made sure Dad had the best care possible, complete with all the medications, supplements, and all the possible examinations he needed. "Dad's good for another ten years," she once announced.

But God had other plans. In 2006 Dad suffered an aneurysm, followed by a heart attack, and passed within four days of the diagnosis. He was deeply mourned by those whose lives had been touched by his generosity and kindness.

It was July 25, 2014, and Dad's eighth death anniversary. I read somewhere that to cherish the memories of a loved one, it would be a good idea to spend the death anniversary doing something that reminded you of the person.

What better way is there to remember Dad than to have a Peking duck dinner? I thought.

On short notice, Paul and I invited family to join us in our celebration. Dad enjoyed Chinese Peking duck with its crispy, deep amber skin and slivers of green onions, drizzled with hoisin sauce and all rolled together like a burrito.

Paul's mom had company that afternoon. She asked, "May I invite Becky? She is coming tonight, and it'll be nice to have her join us for dinner."

"That would be lovely," I responded, happy that we could all go and enjoy the evening.

We had a sumptuous dinner of our favorite Chinese dishes, highlighted with the three-way Peking duck treat. After we had our fill and were leaving the restaurant, Becky came to me and sheepishly asked, "Do you like figs? My tree is just bursting with them, and I have some in the car."

It took me a few seconds to say, "Yes, in fact, I do."

My heart and thoughts were united in knowing that Dad was there with us.

"For we walk by faith, not by sight."
-2 Corinthians 5:7

DAD AND A PRAYER ANSWERED

*Oftentimes we do not comprehend how and why
stories of our lives unfold as they do. Only after
the chapter is finished can we truly understand.*

Dad was diagnosed with Alzheimer's before the turn of the millennium. Slowly but surely, he started experiencing the complications of the ravaging disease. *I prayed that I could spend some time with him before the disease took over him completely.*

A year flew by, and Thanksgiving 2005 was just around the corner. Dad surprised us with a visit to our family in Los Angeles the Monday before Thanksgiving.

The following day, he said, "Book me a return flight to Manila tomorrow. I want to go home." He had no idea of the logistics and thought that Manila was just an hour's flight away. Ingeniously, Paul was able to convince Dad that he needed full and comprehensive medical checkup here in Los Angeles, so we were able to keep him for a little longer.

During his visit, I never felt closer to Dad. I was able to spend quality time with him and care for him. When he left for Manila, I felt a very deep and profound sadness inside that I could not explain. My heart poured itself out to Jesus and sought comfort and solace. *I prayed that whatever happens to Dad, to please let me be with him.*

Around that time, I was homeschooling my seven-year-old son Chris, and his history class was on China. We learned about the terracotta warriors and horses in Xian, China. It was so amazing that about three thousand Chinese stone warriors dating to approximately the third century were discovered in this city. Emperor

Qui Shi Huang, the first emperor of China, had the warriors built to protect him in the afterlife. One of the fascinating things was that the warriors each had a unique facial feature, which made me wonder if they were each sculpted with a warrior in mind.

"I've wanted to visit China for some time now," quipped Paul. We thought this was the best time to travel with the children who were just old enough to enjoy the new sights and appreciate this adventure. Our whole family was so excited just thinking about the Great Wall in Beijing, the terracotta warriors in Xian, and the bustling city of Shanghai.

We started planning around October 2005 and applied for our Chinese visas in February 2006 for a trip in June of that year. Andrew, Chris, and Alex were coming with me to Manila for the first three weeks of our six-week vacation, after which Paul was joining us on the last three weeks beginning on July 16 for the China tour.

"How could a pre-schooler be denied a visa? That's insane!" Paul and I were both appalled to learn that our four-year-old was denied entry to China. They said that since his passport was expiring on August 13, within six months of the visa application, the Chinese embassy would not issue him a visa.

"Oh, well," Paul instructed me, "just make sure you get him a new passport and a Chinese visa in Manila so we could still go."

Christmas holidays filled the households, the New Year fireworks lit the night skies, and before we could even finish our spring cleaning, school was over.

June came, and we were all so excited to arrive in Manila.

The next day, I got in touch with a travel agent and asked her to help us renew Alex's US passport. The travel agent said that there was no assurance we could get the passport back in time because the US embassy was sending the passport back to the US for processing.

"The travel agent can't assure us that Alex's passport will be back in a month," I explained over a long-distance call to Paul, who was still in Los Angeles.

"Plan on somewhere else to go then," he answered.

I updated Paul with the plans, and we settled for a Southeast Asian trip to Singapore and Japan. After inquiring about travel requirements, I learned that Alex's visa would face the same problem in Japan. The agent said he would need to get a new passport. "Just travel to Hong Kong or Singapore where the visa requirements are less stringent," she suggested. When I was booking the Hong Kong trip, the agent asked, "When is your son's passport expiring?"

"August 13," I answered.

"You need to travel by July 13, a month before his passport expires." She said that there is a one-month travel allowance with regard to expiring passports.

But then Paul was scheduled to arrive on July 16. He couldn't take off work earlier, so that didn't work out either.

I called Paul in Los Angeles to explain the situation, and he suggested we cut short our trip to Manila and return to the US. We can still book a trip to Orlando or New York for the rest of his vacation. As I changed our return flight, the airline reservation personnel said that all flights were booked since it was peak season, and we would need to be on the waitlist. But being four in the group, it would not be easy.

"Maybe we can see the other islands in the Philippines we have not gone to, like Cebu or Bohol." I was exasperated with the turn of events and would be happy to just go somewhere outside Manila. "After all, an aunt has been inviting us for the longest time to visit her hometown in Bohol," I thought.

I immediately booked a flight to the island of Bohol, but as I was talking to the travel agent, the radio at the office announced that there was a storm brewing in the Bohol area.

"So what's your refund policy in case of a storm and flights are canceled?" I asked.

"Oh, we don't have a refund policy. You can always rebook your flight," she responded. I sighed.

I could not even remember what happened after the series of incidents. All I could recall was that Paul arrived in Manila the following day, Sunday.

Since we had not planned anything yet, our family visited relatives the first week Paul arrived. Early Friday morning, we got a call that Dad had become disoriented and was brought to the hospital. After a CT scan showed brain hemorrhage, he was confined in the hospital for observation. His condition seemed to improve remarkably the following day Saturday, so Paul and I proceeded to plan an out-of- town trip. "Finally," I told Paul, "we can now plan something."

Nearing midnight of Sunday, we got a call from the hospital saying that Dad had a heart attack. We all rushed to his side, and in two days, he was gone.

Throughout the wake and funeral services, people told me, "How lucky that you and your family were in Manila when your dad passed."

It was then I realized that much as we tried to go somewhere, we could not leave Manila. It was as if someone was making sure we would be in Manila when Dad left us.

It was not luck. It was grace in a prayer answered.

**"If you remain in me and my words remain in you,
ask for whatever you want and it will be done for you."
-John 15:7**

ENCOUNTER AT THE CHAPEL

Have you ever been in a situation where you knew you were placed there for a reason? Let me share this with you.

I was in the Philippines when Mom was scheduled for a medical procedure. Peritoneal line access was going to be put on her as preparation for dialysis. I left ahead for the hospital to arrange her room.

"It's almost noon. Maybe I should grab something from the cafeteria before they arrive," I thought. My brother called to say that they were running a little late. *Well, I can also pray in the chapel.* I deliberated between these two, but the chapel won.

As soon as I seated myself near the chapel entrance in a nearly empty room, I noticed a lady in the row in front of me weeping. As the minutes passed, she became very distraught and emotional. Her sobbing almost became short of hysterical. I felt so bad for her.

"Excuse me," I tapped on her shoulder and asked, "did a family member of yours pass away?" Oftentimes people sought solace in the chapel when things seemed hopeless.

She looked at me, and with unrestrained tears she, narrated to me what happened.

"I went to Philippine General Hospital to bring money to pay for my cancer check-up today, but on the way there, inside the bus, someone slashed my envelope and stole my money." She showed me the slashed plastic folder where she had all her paperwork. "I came here to St. Luke's because I have a friend who worked here. I was going to borrow money from her, but she did not go to work today." Her words were being cut off by her sobbing. "I cannot even go back home to the province."

"How much do you need to go home?"

"Three thousand pesos." (At that time this was about sixty dollars.)

I looked inside my wallet, and all I had was three thousand pesos.

She thanked me profusely and was giving me her earrings, a ring... anything she can find on her and from her bag to give me. I did get the wooden ten bead rosary that she had in her bag as a reminder of this encounter.

I continued praying for her well-being as I left the chapel to attend to Mom.

"But grace was given to each of us according to the measure of Christ's gift."
-Ephesians 4:7

MOM'S LAST NOTE

I miss the days when people wrote cards and letters to each other. I suppose nothing can beat the practicality, efficiency, and speed of today's internet capabilities. But sometimes there is something more to practicality, efficiency, and speed.

"**C**hild, can you please make a draft of what I will write on the card?" requested Mom, her forehead twitching a little frown but her lips hiding a smile.

If generosity were a talent, Mom would win big-time. She had a huge and magnanimous heart but almost a nonexistent talent in writing. As for me, I just wrote whatever was on my mind.

So that was the state of writing affairs during Christmas, birthdays, and other occasions. One time, Mom teased me, "My letters will be rare and priceless because I don't write often."

"Well," I said, totally agreeing with her, "they are definitely more valuable than my letters, which are a penny a dozen because I write to many people."

When I left for the States in the eighties, I continued to write her regularly in the traditional fashion—via snail mail. When the Internet became mainstream, I emailed her. She very rarely wrote back, and so as not to put pressure on her, I ended my letter telling her that no response was needed. And of the very few times that she wrote, I treasured each letter and put them all in a box.

In August 2012, Mom passed away in the Philippines from renal failure due to complications of diabetes. She had a long and difficult final year, and the only thought that eased my pain of loss was to remember that she was in a much better place. (Dad passed away in 2006.)

A couple of weeks passed after her funeral, and I was back in Los Angeles trying to return to my normal daily routine. As I was searching our bedroom drawers for an item for my youngest son's project, I saw an envelope with Mom's handwriting.

It read:

> Dear Paul and Anna,
>> Thank you so much for everything.
>>> Love,
>>> Dad and Mom

It was concise, rare, and precious. And always will be.

"His master said to him,
'Well done, my good and faithful servant.
Since you were faithful in small matters,
I will give you great responsibilities.
Come, share your master's joy."
-Matthew 25:23

DEAD FOR A REASON

Has your cell phone ever stopped working, not just lose charge, when you need it most? Well, it's not something you'd like to happen, especially when you are just about to leave home for some trip far, far away.

"How worse can things get?" I was so frustrated that my cell phone suddenly died as we were leaving the house for the airport. I was going to visit my brother in the Philippines and get some of Mom's belongings after she passed.

Chris, the tech guy in our family, recharged the phone and did all he could to fix the problem.

"Just leave the phone with me," Paul suggested. "If it's not working here, it won't be working there."

"I'll bring it anyway," I countered. "Maybe it'll start working when I get to Manila. Who knows, maybe it needs a vacation too."

"Well," I thought, "in a way, it'll be a blessing that the phone's not working. I can spend quality time with my brother, whom I never really got the chance to know as an adult as we went our separate ways early in our lives." He helped with the family business as I left for the United States in my mid-twenties.

It made me think of Mom. She did not like cell phones. She never had one and never needed one. Whenever I visited her and we were together, it was a no-no to be texting over the phone. She wanted me to spend quality time with her. My presence alone was not quality time. She understood and tolerated calls but texting while I was with her made her feel alone. And she made her feelings known.

When I arrived in Manila, I left the phone to charge, but it still wouldn't work. My brother Joe got me a cell phone to use in Manila, but I didn't need it, because I ended up spending all my time with him.

We talked about everything and anything. I didn't even realize it was time to go back to Los Angeles. I left Manila feeling so happy and yet sad—happy that I was able to spend time with Joe as never before. I also felt connected to Mom through him. He took very good care of Mom those twenty years when I was away raising a family. I felt sad because I wanted more time to spend with him and his family.

"Chris wanted me to get you a new phone, but I wanted to wait until you get back. This way, you can choose a phone that you like," Paul told me as he picked me up from Tom Bradley International Airport.

"Mom, let me have your phone, and I'll charge it one last time before you get a new one," Chris suggested when I got home.

As I was unpacking my luggage, Chris came running to me. "Mom! Your phone's working!" Paul could not believe it until he saw my phone working like nothing happened.

I knew it. Someone wanted me to be able to spend quality time with my brother.

And I did.

"I will praise you with all my heart,
glorify your name forever, Lord my God.
-Psalm 86:12

SUNFLOWER

Mom and I shared an all-time favorite movie, Sunflower, and the movie's wistfully nostalgic theme song "Sunflower" by Henri Mancini. During times when we were together and would hear the song being played, we would smile to each other, knowing that we were enjoying both the song and the movie in our minds.

The movie opened to a field of sunflowers as far as the eye can see. Then came Sofia Loren having a summer fling with Marcelo Mastroianni under the backdrop of World War II tensions in Europe. The two fell in love, and after a few days, got married so she could help him dodge the mandatory draft.

The authorities learned of their plot, and Marcelo was sent to Siberia to fight the Russians. He was found unconscious by a Russian lady who nurtured him to health. Presumably, his amnesia made him forget about Sophia, and he started a family with the Russian lady.

Meanwhile, Sofia was searching for Marcelo all those years looking for him in every far-flung town in Russia until finally, she found his family in a remote village. Marcelo was coming home from work when his eyes met hers. The scene where Sofia looked at Marcelo was too much to bear. It was the most heartbreaking scene I had to endure as a young adult. I became teary-eyed whenever I heard that song, which brought me back to the field of sunflowers.

Dad passed away in 2006, and Mom in 2012. All those years they were still with us, we would spend all of our vacation days visiting them. Mom often told me to skip a year and go to Europe, where Paul would like to travel.

"Let's visit Mom while she's still here with us." Paul was very supportive of our vacation plans every year. Early in life, I learned that touring new places was not as important to me as it was being with loved ones.

After Mom passed away in August 2012, for the very first time, we spent our family summer vacation the following year in Europe. It was what Mom always wanted for us.

On our way to Florence to see Michelangelo's *David*, I was deep in thought, and my heart was still laden with sadness from losing Mom. My head was bowed low, with tears swelling in my eyes, when something turned my head to the window. There before me was a vast field of sunflowers as far as my eyes could see. My heart burst with joy, and the outpouring of tears all came too suddenly. I just felt Mom in my heart and her presence all around me. In my mind, I could hear the movie's theme song playing.

On our return trip, everyone in the bus dozed off from exhaustion, but I stayed awake.

And yet I did not see the field of sunflowers. But it did not matter. Mom was there with me enjoying the sunflowers, the movie, and the song."

"As a mother comforts her child, so I will comfort you;
in Jerusalem you shall find your comfort."
-Isaiah 66:13

COOKING MISHAP

I was frying some egg rolls when the boiling hot oil suddenly splattered before I put on the cover. Several tiny droplets sprayed on my clothes, but a big one landed on my forearm. I instinctively put a cold compress on the quickly reddening area. The following day, a brown discoloration was on my arm, one of many that often reminded me to be careful in the kitchen. Then I remembered my sister-in-law.

Thanksgiving is one of many beautiful, meaningful holidays observed here in the United States. People say it's the most celebrated (and most traveled) festivity as it transcends race, religion, and culture.

In 2004, Paul's sister Carla hosted Thanksgiving. While versed in matters of finance, equities, and real estate at work, she's a specialist in strawberry cheesecake and baked ham at home.

Two evenings before Thanksgiving, Carla called.

"Is Paul there? I want to ask him about an ointment for burns."

"Are you okay?" I didn't think anything was remarkably wrong. Carla said that as she turned the ham in the oven, the boiling oil and juices thrust itself onto her face. I often cook, and oil splattering all over my face, arms, and hands was nothing new. I didn't think anything was serious as she sounded calm, though a restrained kind of calm. I was busy baking and multitasking myself, so I was half aware of what she was saying. I handed the phone to Paul and forgot about the incident.

During Thanksgiving dinner, I noticed that Carla's face was red and had several blisters with large patches of scorched skin on her face and forehead. I did not realize that the burns she sustained were third degree. She mentioned that she saw a dermatologist for her condition the day after the incident.

A couple of weeks later, we had a get-together, and her wounds seemed dry and healing exceptionally well. It was after about a month when I saw her next, and the scars on her face were almost indistinguishable.

I asked her what she did for her wounds to heal that quickly, and she said, "The night of the incident, I was so horrified about the open wounds on my face that after cleaning and putting on the ointment, I fell asleep while incessantly praying. *Please help me, Jesus. Please help me, Jesus. Please help me, Jesus.* From that night and for days after, I said the same prayer silently in my head, over and over again throughout each day until I fell asleep."

She continued, "When I saw my dermatologist the day after the incident, he closely examined my facial burns and calmly relayed to me that it would take about three months to heal but that I would more than likely have burn scars on my face. He then prescribed an antibiotic ointment for my open wounds. After three days, I was out and about feeling quite well, and after five days, I was at work without any gauze pads on my face."

Less than three months after the accident, she has no scars on her face, though the mark on my forearm continues to this day.

"O LORD, my God,
I cried out to you for help and you healed* me."
-Psalm 30:3

THE CENTERPIECE

*Sometimes, we do not even have to pray for things
because our Lord knows our heart's desires.*

I love hosting Christmas dinners! (Now, cleaning up after the party
is another story.) Christmas has such a special place in my heart
that no matter what the situation, we always host this occasion.

I take the time to plan the menu, prepare a program of sorts,
and invite guests who may not have anything planned that evening. I also put in extra effort in arranging the centerpiece for the
buffet table.

Every year, I have a homemade dessert, flowers, fruits, or a
combination of any of those three as our centerpiece.

Last year, I thought it would be appropriate to have a nativity
scene as our centerpiece as Christmas was the occasion we were
celebrating—the birth of our Lord Jesus Christ.

I scouted the gallerias, malls, and specialty home stores for
the right nativity scene. I even looked for one from my mom's
collection of nativity figurines in the Philippines when I visited
earlier that year. None seemed to work. I wanted one that was
about nine inches by nine inches at the base and about six to eight
inches tall. I wanted it to have the Holy Family in a manger and
maybe with some sheep and a shepherd.

A week before Christmas, everyone was so busy with the season's activities that I gave up hope finding my nativity scene. I
opted to place my special Food for the Gods cake, our traditional
Jesus birthday cake, at the center of the buffet table.

"Maybe next year I'll find something if I start looking early
enough." I was a little disappointed at not having my crèche.

December 23 came, and everyone was even busier with their schedules. Even packages that arrived in the mail were put aside.

"You need to open the packages because there might be fresh fruits or something perishable," quipped Paul. I have a habit of opening gifts only when I have the time to appreciate the gift. But Paul was right. I didn't want anything perishable to spoil when I open it on Christmas Day.

My mind wasn't in gift appreciation mode when I was opening the package. Then I felt my heart stop when I saw what was in the box. Carefully wrapped in layers of white tissue was the loveliest wooden nativity scene in a manger in the exact size I wanted, with sheep and a shepherd watching over baby Jesus!

My heart overflowed with joy at the thoughtful gift from my godparents! I was speechless for quite some time as I thanked God for the one gift I wanted so badly that Christmas.

**"Trust in the LORD and do good that you may dwell
in the land and live secure."
-Psalm 37:3**

IMMACULATE HEART RADIO

There are mysterious things in life—circumstances that we cannot explain, like maybe losing matching pairs of socks. We don't know how those happen. This mystery is one of mine.

For the past eight years and into my ninth, I have been driving home from downtown Los Angeles every day, Monday through Friday, at 7:45 a.m. after dropping my sons off to school.

Traffic seems to compound by the minute as everyone is on the road to work. The gridlock starts as soon as one enters Freeway 110. This is the freeway that passes through downtown Los Angeles where Staples Center, Cathedral of Our Lady of the Angels, and the Garment, Flower, and Jewelry Districts are situated.

The same routine is played in the afternoon at pickup time. Around 3:00 p.m. as I get into the car, I turn on the ignition and click the radio button to one of only two stations—news or music.

One afternoon as I was leaving home to pick up my son, I turned on the radio, and it was set to 930 AM.

"Now who would change my station?" I asked myself as I heard the talk show host respond to a listener on the radio. The conversation caught my attention. The talk show host was taking questions from listeners about Catholicism. As I turned on the keys to the ignition, my curiosity turned to a deep interest in the questions being asked. "This is pretty interesting." I was going to listen a few minutes more before I toggle back between my music and news stations.

That was a year ago. Since then, I have seldom gone back to the other stations. It has usually been 930 AM Immaculate Heart

Radio for me. I tell family and friends about the station, and they ask me, "Who introduced you to this station?"

Up to now, I still can't answer that one.

Postscript: Immaculate Heart Radio is now Relevant Radio.

**"Therefore my heart is glad,
my soul rejoices;
my body also dwells secure."
-Psalm 16:9**

DESPERATE FOR GRACE

Desperate is a relative term. One can feel desperate when traffic is so heavy that being late for school is imminent. Or one can feel desperation when there is only one minute left before the store closes on Christmas Eve, and there's one more gift to get. In this story, desperation has a much more serious tone.

Since my mysterious radio station change, my channel has usually been set to Immaculate Heart Radio 930 AM, at home and in the car. I was listening to stories of conversion when I chanced upon this one truly unforgettable story.

The topic of the hour was about God's grace in our lives. The caller was a young man who worked at Marie Callender's Restaurant in Los Angeles, California. He said that he just started employment at the restaurant and was assigned to closing the store. Having just begun a few days back, he had not been given the responsibility of opening or closing the safe, where the sales proceeds were kept for the evening. This task was the responsibility of the manager, who left early that day.

That evening as he was closing, three masked robbers went inside the restaurant and demanded money. The young man said that the money had been locked up by the manager in the safe, and he did not know the combination.

One of the robbers then showed his gun and ordered the young man to open the safe. Despite his repeated explanation that he did not know the numbers, the robber still demanded that he open the safe. When his first and second attempts failed, the robber directed the gun at him and said, "I will kill you if you don't open the safe on the third try."

At that moment, he made a deal with God.

"God, please help me. If I open the safe, I promise I will change my life and devote it to you," whispered the young man under his breath. As he turned the knob, he heard a click, and the safe opened.

He lived to tell this story and lived his life as he promised God.

"Yet when you seek the Lord, your God, from there,
you shall indeed find him if you search after him
with all your heart and soul."
-Deuteronomy 4:29

GOWN IN TIME

—⊙⌾✙⌾⊙—

It never did occur to me, even the slightest chance, that I would one day feel like Cinderella. Well, not exactly in the way that you'd think. Pretty close though.

"I don't want to spend too much for something I'll probably use just once... lucky if I get to use it twice." I was talking to myself as I entered the ladies section of the department store.

"I should have done my shopping earlier. It's also not easy to find a decent gown given my budget." I regretted having put off this shopping.

In April, Paul's niece and her fiancé requested us to be their godparents at their wedding. Time flies by quietly and surprises you with a jolt. It was just a few weeks before their wedding that August.

As I browsed through the rows of formal attire, I envisioned a basic ankle-length dress with an A-line cut. I was hoping to find something uncomplicated to work on, to maybe put some sequins for accent.

I had never bought a gown before. When Mom was alive, she would custom order my clothes here in Los Angeles from her dressmaker in the Philippines. When she passed away, I was just glad that I did not have a big need for a lot of clothes. Then came this surprise special wedding invitation.

As I was about to give up and proceed to another department store, I saw a simple gown in a shade of pink, the bride's color motif. I thought it was too simple, so I planned to sew in some pink sequins to add interest and a touch of elegance.

Upon trying it, I found the gown to be about a size larger. I didn't think that was a problem as I could easily have a dear friend Therese alter it. Therese is a professional alterations specialist here in Los Angeles and is the sister of Mom's dressmaker in the Philippines.

When I called Therese to explain my predicament and to schedule an alteration appointment, she excitedly told me that her sister from the Philippines had a gown custom made there and air freighted here to Los Angeles, only to be returned to her by the client because it did not fit the client who ordered it.

Even after Therese disassembled the gown to loosen the bodice, it still did not fit the client. She suggested that I should try the gown. When I said that the color motif might not be right, all she said was, "I'll go to your house, and let's see if it works."

The moment the chiffon gown went through my head and slid down my body, I truly felt like Cinderella putting on the glass slippers and the shoe fitting her dainty little foot perfectly. The entire bodice of the dress was a perfect fit, and the length didn't even need adjustment. And to top that, the ecru chiffon gown had lovely pink sequined flower patterns that adorned the upper bodice, something I had been planning to put on my purchased gown!

At the wedding mass during the homily, the thought dawned on me, *Could this gown be a gift from Mom?* Tears started to swell up my eyes. Then a realization came to mind—Mom's death anniversary was coming up in four days.

From beyond and after all these years, she was still there to have a dress custom made for me.

"Rejoice in the Lord always. I shall say it again: rejoice!"
-Philippians 4:4

ST. MARY MAGDALENE

This is a beautiful story of redemption in more ways than one.

"**W**hy would any mom name her daughter Magdalene?" I was thinking about my friend Magdalene's mom. Every Christian knows that Mary Magdalene was a prostitute and led an immoral life. *No one would want that name for her daughter,* I thought. It was an unimaginable thing to do.

As I went through college, like most everyone I knew, I dreamt of getting married one day, which I almost did. I got engaged, but very sadly, things didn't proceed as planned. That profound loss led to a haze of relationships that didn't work out either. I now believe I was in a state of confusion about my priorities at that point.

After years of broken relationships and hearts, I sought God's guidance, set things right, and finally chose to settle down to a quiet family life.

It was during the years my children were growing up when I started to look back at my life and felt sorrow for the life I led previously. I *prayed unceasingly* to Jesus for forgiveness and for the people I hurt.

One afternoon while praying by my bedside, I had a vision of a scene that was eerily familiar, unfolding in my mind.

The scene opened with a woman's back in a sparsely lighted room that seemed to come out of ancient times. As the vision continued, I saw that the woman who had long hair seemed to be kneeling beside a partial back view of a man sitting down. Right at that moment, I knew in my heart that the man was Jesus, and I recognized the scene out of the Bible when Mary Magdalene was wiping the feet of Jesus.

The lady slowly and lovingly wiped Jesus's feet. As my vision slowly zoomed closer to the lady, she turned her face toward me and instead of seeing Mary Magdalene's face, I saw mine! *I was the lady washing Jesus's feet!*

I cried unabashedly. I knew and felt at that very precise and precious moment that Jesus had a long time ago already forgiven me.

Then something inside me spoke, *So I tell you, her many sins have been forgiven; hence, she has shown great love. But the one to whom little is forgiven loves little.*[7]

From then on, I have kept St. Mary Magdalene close to my heart, a heart that is now filled with a deep love and respect for this special saint.

Postscript: This story was written based on my personal experience and my interpretation of events.

Recent studies, however, have indicated that St. Mary Magdalene was not the prostitute as she is portrayed in Western art and history. Growing up in the sixties, I learned that she was the same person, hence my attitude towards St. Mary Magdalene was such. The gospel of John related it was Mary of Bethany who anointed the feet of Jesus in the house of Lazarus. In a similar gospel, Luke narrated of a sinner wiping the feet of Jesus with expensive oils in the house of Simon the Pharisee. The two identities were conflated when Pope Gregory's sermon in 1969 identified the two as the same Mary. As to whether it was St. Mary Magdalene whom I saw in my vision, I now believe, is irrelevant. It is only personally relevant because I had looked down on Mary Magdalene in my youth. The main focus is that Jesus forgave the sinner much because she has loved much.[8]

"I tell you, the latter went home justified, not the former;
for everyone who exalts himself will be humbled,
and the one who humbles himself will be exalted."
-Luke 18:14

---

[7] Lk 7:47

[8] Alon Bernstein and Isaac Scharf, "Mary Magdalene Was Not a Prostitute, Scholars Say. This Is What She Really Was," *The Independent*, March 30, 2018, https://www.independent.co.uk/news/world/middle-east/mary-magdalene-feminism-metoo-jesus-disciples-apostle-christianity-judaism-pope-francis-vatican-a8281731.html.

ST. MARTHA

*Taco Tuesdays is a pretty good marketing slo-
gan. I started calling Tuesdays at our home
two ways: T-Mobile Tuesdays for the deals
the phone service carrier has for its custom-
ers and St. Martha Tuesdays for our novena to
this wonderful saint. I easily forget Taco and
T-Mobile Tuesdays but rarely forget the latter.*

I do not remember what I had for breakfast yesterday, but I will
not forget the day I got my St. Martha novena.

I was in high school when I visited the Church of the
Immaculate Conception. Upon kneeling, I noticed a small, folded
white paper on the pew in front of me. I picked it up and saw that
it was a novena to St. Martha. Even before I finished reading the
novena, I was lightly tapped by an elderly lady who seemed to
appear from nowhere. She smiled and nodded at me. I understood
right then that she was the one who placed the novena on the pew.

She whispered to me, "That novena is very powerful," to
which I answered with a question, "Is it effective?" There's not
much substance one can expect from my fifteen-year-old self.

She smiled a lovely smile and left.

As often as I needed help with school exams, projects, and
grades, I would start the novena and sure enough, St. Martha would
intercede for me to Jesus, and my prayers would be answered.
Those prayers began in the seventies and continued for four
decades and counting.

During that period, I moved to the States, raised a family, and
managed a household of three little boys plus one. Every day, like

any other, seemed to be filled with cleaning, laundering, tutoring, and driving. The busyness of my schedule did not leave me much time for anything else other than mostly cooking, something that I pretty much enjoyed doing anyway.

Cook and bake I did! I made Thai, Mexican, Japanese, Spanish, Chinese, Vietnamese, and even California fusion cuisine! A cousin teased me that even my *sinigang* soup (sour soup) was Americanized containing broccoli, spinach, and zucchini instead of *labanos* (daikon), *kangkong (water spinach)*, and *talong* (eggplant), which were the traditional Filipino ingredients.

The stresses of daily living became much lighter whenever I cooked or baked for family and friends. For years I experimented on various ethnic cuisines and invited people to the house to celebrate occasions and no-occasion meals.

Meanwhile, I continued my prayers to St. Martha. This time it was for help with my sons' school work. And it was only about a year ago when I realized that I knew little about St. Martha.

Off to Google and I was able to confirm what I already knew—that she was the sister of Mary and Lazarus and a very close friend of Jesus. She was the sister who was busy with things in the kitchen and preparing things for company, mostly Jesus. The Lord lightly rebuked St. Martha for choosing that busyness part, unlike Mary who chose to spend time with him.

Can you believe what else I learned after reading the article about her? At the end of the article, it mentioned that she is the patron saint of cooks! All these years I was doing what she did during her time, and I did not even have a clue!

Most of all, as I am writing this *now*, I also learn that today is her feast day, July 29!

Isn't that something that after all these years of busyness and cooking, St. Martha has always been with me!

**"May the favor of the Lord our God be ours.
Prosper the work of our hands!
Prosper the work of our hands!"
-Psalm 90:17**

PADRE PIO

Padre Pio was born Francesco Forgione in Pietrelcina, Italy. At age five, he devoted himself to God. He became a priest at age twenty-three. At twenty-nine, he experienced the wounds of Jesus, the stigmata—a sacrifice he carried for fifty years. He was blessed with visions and conversations with Jesus and Mother Mary, with knowing the hearts of people, bilocation, healing, miracles, and prophecy. Long before Karol Jozef Wojtyla would become Pope John Paul II, Padre Pio told him that he would one day hold the highest position in the (Catholic) Church.

It was announced weeks ahead during mass that the relics of Padre Pio will be on display at the Holy Family Church in Pasadena, California. I had several appointments that day and would have had to squeeze my visit to Holy Family into my schedule.

For many years, I had been in awe of this pious saint. The life he led was a story on enduring suffering for the sinners of this world. A holy man, he was endowed with the wound marks of Jesus on the cross. He asked that the visible wounds be taken away from him, but not the pain and agony he had to endure with the stigmata. As I read more about him, my reverence for this saint grew deeper.

When I arrived at 9:00 a.m. on the day of the special exhibit and mass for Padre Pio, I learned that I came in too early. The exhibit would be open to the public after the 10:00 a.m. mass.

"Oh no," I sadly realized, "I won't be able to see the relics."

As I started to leave for my appointment, someone tapped my arm. I was astonished to see an aunt.

"Why don't you stay here beside me for mass?" Auntie Dee was inviting me to join her as the church was slowly filling up for Padre Pio's special mass.

Much as I wanted to, I couldn't. "Auntie, I have appointments and can't stay. Thank you so much."

Later that day, I received a text from Auntie Dee containing pictures of the relics of Padre Pio. A few weeks later, I received an envelope containing a beautiful rosary bracelet that was placed beside Padre Pio's relics, a surprising, heartwarming, and touching gift from Auntie and Padre Pio.

"Consider it all joy, my brothers,
when you encounter various trials..."
-James 1:2

ST. THERESE OF THE CHILD JESUS

St. Therese of the Child Jesus was born Marie Francoise-Therese Martin on January 2, 1873. She is also known as "The Little Flower of Jesus" because she describes herself as a flower for Jesus. On her deathbed, she promised that she would "spend her heaven doing good on earth... will let fall from heaven a shower of roses."

I remember praying to St. Therese early in life because I wanted to see if she really sent roses. And she did! If the request were going to be granted, if guidance were going to be shown, or if questions were to be answered in the affirmative, she would let me know.

(I have to admit, though, that in my young adulthood, there were many times I sought her advice, and yet I was not ready to follow through. It took me many, many years to grow into spiritual maturity that would lead me to have complete trust and faith in divine assistance.)

There have been numerous roses sent my way, especially during my younger years. When I got married and started a family, my devotion to St. Therese tapered to nullity.

Decades passed. Only the past couple of months when decisions needed a lot of guidance did I remember St. Therese and start seeking her intercession again.

Just recently, there was a huge project that Paul and I wanted to embark on, but we were not sure if it was something that Jesus would want us to get involved.

"St. Therese, please let me know if this project is something that will make Jesus happy," I prayed. The following day, I received a dozen roses from an acquaintance who just thought I would enjoy some flowers.

"St. Therese, do you think I should submit this manuscript to Christian Faith Publishing?" For the first time at our Legion of Mary meeting the following day, someone put fresh roses on the vase and who do you think cleared the vase after the meeting? Yes, I did. Looking back, I was aghast that I even threw the fresh roses in the trash, forgetting all about my novena to St. Therese.

The most recent wonderful grace she bestowed upon me was when our family was able to go to Europe for our 25th wedding anniversary.

A week before our trip, an aunt called to ask me if we were going to see the Basilica of St. Therese in Lisieux, France.

"No, I believe that the city is way farther inside France, and our itinerary is along the coast," I answered.

Three days before our trip, a cousin asked me the same question, and I answered the same.

Then I received a St. Therese card that week. I started to wonder, *"Is St. Therese telling me something?"*

The evening before our trip, I looked at the map and was astounded to learn that her basilica is just an hour ride from another city that we were visiting!

So we took a taxi to St. Therese Basilica in Lisieux, and as we alighted from the car, a light shower greeted us. It took all of 30 seconds for the shower to drizzle our jackets.

Then an amazing feeling of visiting an old friend's house overwhelmed me. I knew right there that St. Therese welcomed us to her home.

"As for the holy ones who are in the land,
they are noble, in whom is all my delight."
-Psalm 16:3

OUR LADY OF LOURDES

The Blessed Virgin Mary appeared to a young girl named Bernadette Soubirous on February 11, 1858, at a grotto near Lourdes, France.

Though belief in these apparitions is not a necessity for Catholic faith, in my opinion, all Catholics believe that Our Lady did appear to Bernadette.[9]

A year before our milestone occasion, Paul asked, "Where would you like to go if we could go on a trip for our twenty-fifth wedding anniversary?"

It didn't take me a second to respond, "To France to visit the shrine of Our Lady of Lourdes as a family, and to Portugal, to visit Our Lady of Fatima because it is the hundredth anniversary of her apparition. You know we've often asked the Blessed Mother for help in our prayers to Jesus."

Early on in my married life, I knew I was going to visit Lourdes someday. Paul and I were both born on her feast day, February 11.

I did my research and asked around for suggestions on how we should proceed with our trip. We consulted family and friends who were experts on traveling, and they were unanimous in suggesting that land tours for pilgrimages were the way to go. The

[9] As vested by the Council of Trent, local bishops have the authority to recognize apparitions in their respective areas. See Michael O'Neill, "The Miracle Hunter : Approved Apparition Claims," The Miracle Hunter, 2015, http://www.miraclehunter.com/marian_apparitions/approved_apparitions/vatican.html.

tours would be complete with daily masses and rosary prayers. I told them our boys would much rather enjoy a cruise, but the answer was a consensus: there was no way I could find a cruise that will bring us to the Lourdes Shrine.

Paul and I met in 1990, and we now are a family of five with three sons. Our oldest son had just started a job and would not be able to join us.

As I was looking into the various tours to Lourdes, I sought guidance and prayed, *"Mother Mary, I would like to bring my family to you. You've always helped me pray to Jesus. Please assist me in planning a trip that will work for everyone in our family, in Jesus's name."*

Six months had passed, and we welcomed 2017.

"Have you found a trip already?" Paul was reminding me that there wasn't much time left to plan our trip.

Mid-January, I began to panic as flight and tour prices had started their ascent as the summer months were already on the horizon. After looking at several sites, I stumbled upon a cruise company's itinerary in the Iberian Peninsula. As I looked into the details, I realized that the cruise disembarks at Gijon, Spain, a port that is just a four-and-a-half-hour drive from Lourdes, France. And to add to this streak of "luck," the ship continued to the next port Bilbao, Spain, which was just two hours away from Gijon.

If only I could find a driver who could take us to Lourdes, stay there overnight, and then return us to Bilbao port, then all will be well, I thought. I was getting excited as the cruise would be a boon to our sons who love cruising.

I had to find the drivers first before booking the cruise. I found a wonderful Internet travel site that connected me with European escorts and drivers. I e-mailed five drivers early dawn. My excitement was getting the better of me when the response from the first driver the following morning dampened my enthusiasm. He said that the region I wanted was not within his area, so he declined.

Due to some baffling circumstances, I could not access the other drivers' responses the following days as my connection to the site could not go through. It instructed me to change my password repeatedly and to wait for their e-mail to reset it. I went back to the site numerous times as instructed, but their site just wasn't accessible anymore.

At this point, I was getting very anxious and wondering why things weren't working out as easily as I thought. As a desperate move, I called an uncle who knew a driver in Rome.

"Uncle, do you think your driver will be able to drive us to Lourdes from Bilbao, Spain?"

"I don't think he will do that because he is based in Rome and that's pretty far from France." I got the driver's contact information anyway and e-mailed him.

It seemed a pretty long wait, but on the evening of February 10, the driver e-mailed me back, "I don't make long-distance trips, but I will do this trip *just for you.*"

I cried. I knew it was Our Lady of Lourdes assisting me. It was the day before her feast day.

I was finally able to book our cruise, which included a side trip to Lourdes, a combination that family and friends said was likely not possible.

A month before our trip, our oldest son called. He said that he would be able to join us on our trip!

On the night of our stay at the Shrine of Our Lady of Lourdes, I had my entire family together.

It was a dream come true.

"And Mary said: 'My soul proclaims
the greatness of the Lord;
my spirit rejoices in God my savior,
For he has looked upon his handmaid's lowliness;
behold, from now on will all ages call me blessed.'"
-Luke 1:46-48

RHEMA, A GODSENT

How does one give thanks for an awe-inspiring, amazing gift? I believe that there is only one way: to share the story of how the blessing was given.

Of our twenty-two years of marriage, about eighteen years of those Sunday afternoons have been spent going to open houses. "Lookie-loos," they called people like us. But we carried that label a notch higher. Paul and I enjoyed looking at the home's style, the curb appeal, architecture, and how the interiors were decorated. We rated the homes, discussed which parts of the house we like, assessed if the pricing was on target, and evaluated the potential of a home. Mind you, we were very picky lookie-loos. Finally, we would ask each other if we liked a house enough (within our price range) to leave our current house.

During open house, we were often asked if we were in the real estate profession. We were also laughed at because agents already knew us as "the couple who will never buy a home." We had been happy and content with our house, so there was no real desire or urgency to move.

One Sunday afternoon, we were driving to the nearby city of La Cañada when we saw a sign along our regular route.

"Hey, there's an open house," Paul said. My answer was the usual, "Let's take a look."

Upon seeing the façade, I sighed. "I saw this house on the Internet, and it's way beyond our price range."

"Well, we're here already… might as well look." Paul parked the car amongst the dozens of cars parked along the street.

Entering the front door, we saw an elegantly adorned traditional with sparse but well-thought-out refined classic furniture. A few paces and we saw the lovely views of the San Fernando Valley come out from the living room windows. A couple more steps and we were treated to the expansive views of downtown Los Angeles, Eagle Rock, and Universal City from the sunroom.

In all these years of looking, we have only seen a handful of properties with comparable views and wrap-around ample yard space. Our hearts fluttered with the thought that we could live in a house like this.

"Is the price negotiable?" I asked the listing agent Celine who gave me a surprised look and said, "Not really. This house just came to the market."

"That house," she continued as she pointed to the neighbor's house, "just sold in May for an amount close to this asking price."

Our excitement gave way to reality when the realtor said the price was firm and not open to negotiation. As we went around the home, we noticed statuettes of the Blessed Virgin Mary with Jesus and a saint or two. *Oh, the residents are Catholic*, I thought.

Back at home that evening, Paul and I could not help but think of the lovely home with the awesome views. The following days were the same: we would talk about the house incessantly.

"I'll call Celine and ask permission if we can look at the backyard again," I told Paul. The house was vacant as the owner moved to a care home. I called the agent and being the nice and accommodating person that she is, she said, "No problem."

The following day after work, I met Paul at the property. During this second visit, we passed by the right side gate, and guess who seemed to welcome us? A statue of St. Francis of Assisi seemed to greet those who used the gate.

"St. Francis," I called to him like a friend. "It's October 4 today, your feast day! Do you have a surprise for me?" My thoughts were teasing.

The next four weeks or so, I would call the agent about three times a week to ask permission to see the property and enjoy the magnificent views. (Celine said I called her every day.)

During our visits, we saw the transformation of the setting sun from a light yellow lemon crème to a tint of orange as October came and went. November splashed a deeper tone of orange with streaks of a light reddish hue.

As the days grew shorter and the nights set in earlier, we gasped at the breath-taking beauty of the views, even more, when the lights started coming out of the city, until the entire expanse was one dark canvas speckled with lights from downtown Los Angeles to the surrounding cities. The blackish depths of the shadowy skies were adorned with stars peering out simultaneously with flickering lights from airplanes waiting for their turn to land at the Los Angeles and Burbank airports.

One afternoon as we were enjoying the views, Celine came to show the house to another client. She asked us, "Would you like to make an offer?"

"Well, we cannot really afford it. Our budget is only so much," we responded. "We just wanted to enjoy the place while we still can."

"Well, that offer is on the low side. We already have six offers on the table."

"You know how much we love the house, and every day I pray that if the house is for us, for God to please grant it to us. But if it is not, to please *not* give it to us."

I once told Paul that I did not want to live in a house with these extraordinary views as it reminded me of the Temptation in the Desert. In this story, Satan brought Jesus to a hilltop and told Jesus that all the land he (Jesus) can see would be his (Jesus's) if he (Jesus) worshiped him (Satan). I don't want to have a place if that will only remind me of the temptation.

We thanked the agent and went home.

Another week passed by when Celine called, "Why don't you just put in your offer?" Paul and I thought we didn't have anything to lose, so we did.

That weekend, Paul and I went back to the property. I sighed, "This may be the last time we will get to see these views." And then suddenly, a very light shower drizzled upon us. "You know, Paul, I always thought that showers are blessings from heaven."

In three days, we got the call we will never forget, "You got the house!"

Postscript: After we got the home, we were talking to Celine and said that we were drawn to her open house sign on Mountain Street. She said she never put up a sign because she didn't plan on having an open house until the last minute. We knew for sure we saw a sign, but it did not lead us to the other agent's house. It led us to Celine's house.

A few months later, a dear friend texted me and said, "I thought of you the moment our church lector sent us an attachment. I'm sending it to you to read." The attachment said that Rhema in Greek meant "word of God." Our street name is …

RHEMA.

**"What eye has not seen, and ear has not heard,
and what has not entered the human heart,
what God has prepared for those who love him."
-1 Corinthians 2:9**

THANKSGIVING DAY

One of the most valuable things I learned from my mom, which she learned from her mother, is giving thanks. Always. Give thanks for small things, big things, and for one's state of being, whatever it may be. I know it is not easy, especially when things are not going well, but I have heard of circumstances turning around with just living a life of thanksgiving.

It was our second year in the home God gave us.

Someone said that we finally got the house of our dreams. I told her, "No, this is not the house of our dreams. This house is beyond our dreams."

From almost every room, one can see views of downtown Los Angeles to the San Fernando Valley. Guests have commented on how we must have seen the ocean from our backyard. I told them that's what people have been telling us, but so far, we have not seen the ocean yet. I don't even know how the ocean would look from this far. We were about thirty miles from the nearest beach. Homes for sale higher up on the mountains were advertised with ocean views. Not ours. Though I'm not one to desire an ocean view, I have to admit I've climbed on chairs and ladders and stretched a neck to search for a sliver sight of the ocean but never saw it.

One afternoon while driving through the hills from the adjacent city of La Cañada, my eyes were enjoying the beauty of downtown Los Angeles skyline on a clear day when a glimmering sight took my breath away.

"Paul, look!" I pointed to him the shimmering view of the Pacific Ocean. So that's how the ocean looks like. Nope. We had not seen anything like that from our backyard.

Weeks passed. I was lighting my candles by the kitchen window and giving thanks to Jesus, the Blessed Virgin Mary, and the saints just as I do every morning after waking up when all of a sudden, an amazing, glimmering sight greeted me! It was the Pacific Ocean welcoming Thanksgiving Day 2015!

Couldn't have had a better Thanksgiving morning. Ever.

And that was the only time the ocean has presented itself to us. Never again to this day.

"My mouth shall be filled with your praise,
shall sing your glory every day."
-Psalm 71:8

FINAL WORDS

I believe that God's graces are evident in everyone's lives, but only when people open their hearts to him and accept the extraordinary will people see them.

When I started writing these stories, I thought I had some forty stories. I was amazed that as I wrote them down, more stories of grace from years past seemed to present themselves to me. Long before I even finished this manuscript, I almost had enough stories to fill another compilation! The more I also shared with other people, the more people shared their stories with me. The more I believed, the more I recall the graces that have been shown to me. And the more I opened my heart to God, the more graces were bestowed.

It is my wish that your hearts were warmed, touched by these stories, or that you were inspired to see God's grace in your lives.

Maybe looking back on your life, you will find familiar events that happened to you. Please make a note of these events, and in time, you will start to feel a growing presence of God's grace in your lives. With God in your life, you will start your journey toward inner peace and happiness.

Blessings to you on an amazing journey!

WORKS CITED

Alexander, Eben. *Proof of Heaven: A Neurosurgeon's Journey into the Afterlife*. First Edition. New York: Simon & Schuster, 2012.

Bernstein, Alon, and Isaac Scharf. "Mary Magdalene Was Not a Prostitute, Scholars Say. This Is What She Really Was." *The Independent*, March 30, 2018. https://www.independent.co.uk/news/world/middle-east/marymagdalene-feminism-metoo-jesus-disciples-apostle-hristianityjudaism-pope-francis-vatican-a8281731.html.

Lafferty, K. (1974). Seek Ye First. *The Praise Album*. Retrieved from https://www.hymnal.net/en/hymn/ns/120.

Neal, Mary C. *To Heaven and Back: A Doctor's Extraordinary Account of Her Death, Heaven, Angels, and Life Again: A True Story*. First Edition. Colorado Springs: WaterBrook, 2012.

O'Neill, Michael. "The Miracle Hunter : Approved Apparition Claims." The Miracle Hunter, 2015. http://www.miraclehunter.com/marian_apparitions/approved_apparitions/vatican.html.

"Petak and Elahi - NORTHRIDGE EARTHQUAKE, USA.Pdf." Accessed May 21, 2018. http://resilience.abag.ca.gov/wp-content/documents/resilience/toolkit/The%20Northridge%20Earthquake%20and%20its%20Economic%20and%20Social%20Impacts.pdf.

Petak, William J, and Shirin Elahi. "The Northridge Earthquake, USA and Its Economic and Social Impacts." *EuroConference on Global Change and Catastrophe Risk Management Earthquake Risks in Europe, IIASA, Laxenburg Austria, July 6-9, 2000,* 2001, 28.

Provincial Government of Bulacan, Philippines. "Bulacan, Philippines: Bocaue, Bulacan: History." Bulacan, 2007. https://www.bulacan.gov.ph/bocaue/history.php.

Reuter, S. J. Fr James B. *Mama Mary and Her Children (Book 3): True Stories of Real People.* Mama Mary and Her Children 3. Mandaluyong City: Anvil Publishing, Inc., 2011.

*If you feel that the stories here have inspired you
to grow in faith, please consider sharing and
gifting this book to family and friends.*

*If you have stories of grace that you feel will inspire others
to grow in faith, please send your stories to touchedbygrace.
today or to anna.maria.deguid@gmail.com.*

All profits of this book will benefit local,
national, and international charities.

Your support will help bring God to people's
lives. Thank you very much.

ABOUT THE AUTHOR

Anna Maria De Guid resides in Los Angeles. She is married to Paul De Guid, and they have three sons.

While raising a family, she kept busy with school and church activities, as well as cooking and baking. Her venture into writing couldn't have come at a better time. Her role as a homemaker started winding down when her children started going to college. From nourishing tummies, she is now nourishing souls.

CPSIA information can be obtained
at www.ICGtesting.com
Printed in the USA
FSHW020511030220
66763FS

9 781643 496771